What Determines International Competitiveness of the Economy?

Polish Studies in Economics

Edited by Ryszard Kokoszczyński

Volume 12

PETER LANG

Piotr Dybka

What Determines International Competitiveness of the Economy?

Evidence from Bayesian Model Averaging

PETER LANG

Bibliographic Information published by the Deutsche Nationalbibliothek
The Deutsche Nationalbibliothek lists this publication in the Deutsche Nationalbibliografie; detailed bibliographic data is available in the internet at http://dnb.d-nb.de.

Library of Congress Cataloging-in-Publication Data
A CIP catalog record for this book has been applied for at the Library of Congress.

This work was supported by research subvention at SGH Warsaw School of Economics no. KAE/S21.

This work has been reviewed by Marek A. Dąbrowski (Cracow University of Economics) and Piotr Wdowiński (University of Łódź).

ISSN 2191-8848
ISBN 978-3-631-85651-2 (Print)
E-ISBN 978-3-631-85815-8 (E-PDF)
E-ISBN 978-3-631-87358-8 (EPUB)
DOI 10.3726/b19435

Peter Lang – Berlin · Bern · Bruxelles · New York · Oxford · Warszawa · Wien

This publication has been peer reviewed.

www.peterlang.com

Abstract

This study examines three measures of the international competitiveness of the country. The results of the current account analysis indicate that intratemporal factors seem to have a lesser effect than intertemporal factors and therefore a permanent (stable) adjustment of the current account balance requires changes in the factors related to economic development and is a time-consuming, gradual process. There are some profound differences between developing and developed countries in terms of the current account drivers. High-income countries are, to a larger extent, financing investment and government expenditures with external resources, whereas the quality of institutions played a more pronounced role than in the case of developed countries.

Next, I have examined potential determinants of export performance. The observed effects can be divided into two types: direct and transformational effects. The first category includes situations, where improvement of the investigated measure directly stimulates exports, whereas the second type of the impact leads to structural changes (improvement leads to shifting from less to more technologically advanced exports). Obtained results show that technological factors have a much more significant impact on the export market share than price factors. Furthermore, institutions also play an essential role in shaping the international position of the exporters.

Last but not least, I have studied the importance of macroeconomic variables for exchange rate movements. The set of crucial macroeconomic variables for exchange rate movements analysis include terms of trade, general government debt and the GDP per capita. Moreover, the recent Great Recession and the European sovereign debt crisis saw a substantial increase in the volatility in the exchange rates that also lead to some structural changes in the crucial determinants of the currency movements. As a result, exchange rate determinants can substantially differ both in time and across the countries.

Contents

Acknowledgements

I want to thank the following people, without whom I would not have completed this research. Chapter 3 is based on the article Dybka and Rubaszek (2017) that I have written together with Professor Michał Rubaszek from SGH Warsaw School of Economics, whereas in chapter 4, I have used the results from article Bierut and Dybka (2021), published together with Beata Bierut. In addition to this, I would like to thank the Reviewers, Professor Marek A. Dąbrowski and Professor Piotr Wdowiński, for many valuable comments that substantially improved the overall quality of the book. Last but not least, I would also like to thank the Editor, Professor Ryszard Kokoszczyński, for his valuable remarks. Moreover, the book would not have been written without the encouragement from my wife, my parents and my grandparents.

This work was supported by a research subvention at SGH Warsaw School of Economics No. KAE/S21.

1 International competitiveness of countries

The goal of this book is to establish what determines *international competitiveness of countries* and to investigate the veracity of several prospective answers to that question. The first possible source of international competitiveness can stem from the relative price channel. According to this hypothesis, the increase in prices would lead to a deterioration of international competitiveness of a country. Although this explanation seems to be very intuitive, it does not account for the variety of other plausible sources of international competitiveness. The price itself might not be the crucial factor that decides whether a country strengthens its international position. The second potential source of competitiveness results from technological capacity and the quality of human capital of a country. From a more general perspective, investments that lead to the technological or educational transformation of the economy can also be a vital source of (comparative) advantage. As a result, factors affecting decisions on investment and savings, such as credit availability or general government debt or budget balance, can also have a profound impact on international competitiveness. Another compelling hypothesis focuses on the importance of institutions quality. Last but not least, establishing the critical determinants of international competitiveness poses another important research question: is there a universal set of its determinants for all the countries. It might be the case that vital determinants of international competitiveness among the developed countries are somewhat different from those in emerging economies.

From the technical point of view, I attempt to understand international competitiveness of the countries within the panel data regression framework. Using panel data allows comparison not only between the countries but also observing the differences in their relative positions in time. As a result, it enables the identification of factors that shape international competitiveness, because one can observe countries that managed to improve their position. Since the economic literature provides different explanations regarding the critical determinants of international competitiveness of a country, I propose the Bayesian model averaging (BMA) framework for the purposes of this analysis. The main advantage of the BMA approach is that it allows to estimate all the possible models for the given combinations of available variables instead of a single model. For each model in the BMA framework, there is a posterior probability measure that this model reflects the true data generating process. On this basis, I can also obtain the posterior inclusion probability for each variable, which is a straightforward measure of variables' importance. The details of this approach are presented in chapter 2.

The selection of competitiveness measures and identification of its potential determinants requires understanding what the competitiveness is. The main problem is that international competitiveness is extremely hard to define in the context of a country Boltho (1996). Some definitions of international competitiveness focus on productivity. For example, the World Economic Forum writes that economic competitiveness is "the set of institutions, policies and factors that determine the level of productivity of a country."[1] However, it might be argued that this definition is not complete. For example, Fagerberg (1988) noted that a country cannot increase its productivity per se, so it focuses on the realisation of economic policy goals, such as increasing GDP or employment levels.

Economists such as Magaziner and Reich (1982); Tyson (1992); Reich (1992) view competitiveness through a mercantilist lens, which means that the whole economy can be viewed in the same way as a company. In such a case, each country is competing against other countries and aiming at increasing the trade surpluses that are viewed as a country (and losses can be measured in terms of trade deficits). In this framework, a persistent trade deficit leads to the deindustrialisation of the economy. For example, a surge in imported manufactured goods results a decline in manufacturing employment (as the work is shifted towards other countries) and real wages. A potential solution to the country's competitiveness would be an industrial policy that encourages the active role of the government related to funding for education and worker training programs and increasing cooperation between the government and the private sector.

In addition to this, there is also a strand of literature that focuses on exchange rates that could be a simpler way of increasing the price

---

1 https://www.weforum.org/agenda/2017/09/what-is-economic-competitiveness/.

competitiveness of the economy Dornbusch (1996). The key question remains whether the devaluation of the domestic currency can be an effective tool of economic policy? In theory, devaluation of domestic currency should support the exporters (as their products become cheaper) and reduce imports (see, e.g. Chinn, 2006, for a discussion of competitive devaluations).

In contrast, Krugman (1994) calls the international competitiveness a "dangerous obsession." Krugman (1996) criticises the mercantilist approach, as counties do not act in the same way as firms. If a firm consistently incurs losses, then it will go out of business. However, persistent trade deficits do not mean that a country goes bankrupt. A trade deficit may result from an increase in the demand for all goods in a growing economy, both domestically produced and foreign-produced (imports). Nevertheless, the main concern resulting from focusing on external economic performance is that it can lead to wrong economic policies, such as embracing protectionism or promoting their own firms at the expense of other countries' producers Krugman (1996).

Nevertheless, concerning on other economic issues (such as inflation, budget deficits etc.) can also lead to wrong policies and therefore I believe that understanding the factors that affect external balances of the economy can lead to better understanding the overall economic condition and help in developing reasonable policies that support further growth. Moreover, the problems with international competitiveness often are the result of poor structural policies, Llewellyn (1996). Focusing on the economic policy goals, in turn, creates another challenge, which is avoiding macroeconomic imbalances that could lead to a destabilisation of an economy. The discussion on the importance of macroeconomic imbalances leads to the first measure of competitiveness analysed in this book, namely the current account balance. In my opinion, it is the most general measure, as it describes whether a country increases or decreases its net international investment position. The second analysed measure is more specific and is based on the export market share, defined as the share of exports of a given economy in the value of global exports. I chose this measure as it becomes increasingly important due to the growing trade openness of economies (understood as the value of their trade in relation to GDP) resulting from globalisation. The exchange rate is the last competitiveness variable analysed in this work. It can be viewed as a measure directly connected to the relative price channel mentioned at the beginning of this chapter.

In this study, I have used different databases in each chapter focusing on a particular measure of international competitiveness. On the one hand, such an approach makes direct comparisons between the results of each chapter more challenging. On the other hand, it does have some essential advantages. First, it allows the use of the most extensive dataset available, rather than estimating on the basis of largest common sample, which yields a more precise estimate. Second, such an approach also shows which conclusions can be generalised and which depend on additional factors. As a result, I have performed a sensitivity analysis of my results that allows discussion regarding the stability of the results. Third, even though baseline results in each chapter were obtained on the basis of different samples, there are some additional results presented in the sensitivity analysis that make comparisons easier. For example, comparing the results obtained on a broad panel of countries in the case of the analysis of the determinants of the current account with the results on the competitiveness of exports in the European Union countries is difficult. Nevertheless, chapter 3 also contains the results for the sub-sample of economically developed countries to which all European Union countries belong.

The structure of this book is as follows. In chapter 2, I present the methodology applied in this work. The chapter begins with an introduction of the Bayesian model averaging (BMA) framework and discussion of the key assumptions related to the choice of the estimator and the prior size of the model. Next, the interpretation of the BMA results is shown on the basis of exemplary results. Last but not least, I present additional extensions of the BMA framework that were also used in this dissertation.

Chapter 3 focuses on the determinants of the current account. The results indicate that the investment rate, budget balance and relative stage of development can be viewed as the key drivers of the current account. On the other hand, relative prices seem to have a lesser effect on the dependent variable. Another important conclusion from this part of book is that there are differences between developing and developed countries in terms of what drives the current account. High-income countries are, to a larger extent, financing investment and government expenditures with external resources. This stipulates that they have better access to international financial markets.

In turn, for developing countries, the quality of institutions was found to play a more pronounced role than in the case of developed countries.

Chapter 4 focuses on the determinants of the export market share. Regression results show that technological factors exert a much greater impact on export performance than price factors. Moreover, technological factors can have both a direct positive effect on exports as well as a transformational impact, i.e. leading to a change from less to more technologically advanced exports. I also present strong evidence that institutions are vital determinants of export performance that can have both a direct positive effect on exports as well as a transformational impact (from less to more technologically advanced production).

Chapter 5 analyses what determines the exchange rate. Obtained results confirm that variables often used in the behavioural equilibrium exchange rate framework, such as the terms of trade, general government debt and the GDP per capita are indeed essential determinants of the real exchange rate movements. In addition to this, I also study if determinants of exchange rates can differ in time.

Finally, chapter 6 summarises the dissertation. In general, the answer to the main research question is that the crucial determinant of international competitiveness is a good economic policy. Increasing international competitiveness is a gradual process that requires institutional and technological changes rather than a short-term adjustments as the price factors have a very limited effect.

2 Econometric methodology

In this dissertation the dominant framework is based on panel regressions. Using panel data allows for the comparison not only across countries but also observing the differences in their relative positions in time. Moreover, the economic literature provides different explanations regarding the critical determinants of the international competitiveness of the country. Therefore, a single model might not suffice to provide the right answer. As a result, I apply the Bayesian model averaging (BMA) framework for the purposes of this analysis. I refer to BMA as a set of techniques that enable to account for model uncertainty, i.e. the uncertainty related to the selection of variables included in the model. The main advantage of the BMA approach is that I estimate all the possible models for the given combinations of the available variables instead of a single model. For each model in the BMA framework, there is a posterior probability measure that this model reflects the true data generating process. On this basis, I can also obtain the posterior inclusion probability of each variable, which is a straightforward measure of the variable importance.

2.1 BMA framework

The general idea of BMA is to combine the result from all the models that can be estimated on the basis of the available dataset. For example, BMA framework can be used to calculate the average result of panel data regressions:

$$y_{i,t} = \mu_i + \boldsymbol{x}_{j,i,t}^T \beta_j + \varepsilon_{j,i,t} \tag{1}$$

where $\boldsymbol{x}_{j,i,t}$ represents the matrix of explanatory variables included in model *j* for a country *i* in time *t* and β_j denotes the coefficients estimated in model *j*. The $\varepsilon_{j,i,t}$ denotes error term in model *j*. The dependent variable $y_{i,t}$ remains the same in all the averaged models.

The aim of the BMA is to compute the posterior probability of model *j*, denoted as $P(M_j \mid Y)$. This probability is conditional on the marginal likelihood of the model *j*, $p(Y \mid M_j)$, prior beliefs regarding the probability of the model j, $P(M)$, as well as marginal likelihoods and prior probabilities of the remaining models. The formula for the posterior probability is:

$$P\left(M_j|Y\right)=\frac{p(Y\mid M_j)P\left(M_j\right)}{\sum_{k=1}^{2^K}p(Y\mid M_k)P\left(M_k\right)} \tag{2}$$

where Y is the available information set. The number of models assessed in the BMA framework is equal to 2^K, which is the number of possible combinations of K explanatory variables. In this chapter, I will focus on those aspects of the BMA methodology that are related to the panel data regression, however, there is a large number of potential extensions of the BMA framework. Steel (2017) provides an extensive survey of different types of models combined with the use of the BMA framework as well as the prior assumptions taken in the BMA framework.

2.2 Estimation within the BMA framework

The first important decision within the BMA framework relates to the method of calculating the marginal likelihood function $p(Y|M_j)$. For example, in the seminal paper that introduced BMA to broader use in economics, Sala-I-Martin et al. (2004) used the classical Least Squares (LS) estimator and called their approach Bayesian Averaging of Classical Estimates (BACE). Here, I will also use the least squares estimator, however with some modifications described below.

2.2.1 Fixed effects panel regression with *Zellner's g-prior*

Due to the heterogeneity in the sample of analysed countries the least squares estimator has to include an element taking into account the individual characteristics of the countries in the sample. The first choice is usually the so-called fixed effect, i.e. adding country-specific constants into the analysis. In the context of the BMA it can be done in two ways: by including country-specific constants that are always included in the analysis (i.e. I assume that their inclusion probability is equal to 1) or by demeaning of data. This approach can be further extended by adding a Bayesian aspect to the estimation through a set of assumptions called *Zellner's g-prior* (Zellner,

1986). This approach allows researchers adding their prior beliefs regarding the values of the regression coefficients β_j.

In the first step of the *Zellner's g-prior* estimation, I assume that each model *j* has the error term:

$$\varepsilon_t \sim N\left(0, \sigma^2 I\right) \tag{3}$$

To be agnostic, I assume *a priori* that each coefficient is equal to 0, which means that the data itself must show that the variable is significant and can be treated as a determinant of the analysed variable. Moreover, I assume that parameters β_j have the following variance-covariance structure:

$$\beta_j \mid g \sim N[0, \sigma^2 \left(\frac{1}{g} X_j^T X_j\right)^{-1} \tag{4}$$

where X_j is the vector of regression *j* variables. Equation 4 shows that the variance-covariance structure resembles the Least squares estimator and the only difference is the *g* parameter. The low value of the *g* parameter indicates that the researcher is convinced the coefficients of the regression should be close to 0. This would be a conservative approach, as the data must strongly "speak" to convince the researcher that the coefficient value is different from 0. The resulting posterior distribution of β_j coefficients is:

$$E\left(\beta_j | g, X_j, M_j\right) = \frac{g}{1+g} \beta_j \tag{5}$$

Equation (5) also confirms that setting lower values of the *g* parameter would result in the coefficient value closer to 0. Last but not least, the marginal likelihood function can be written as:

$$p(y \mid M_j) \propto (1+g)^{\frac{n-1-K_j}{2}} \left[1 + g\left(1 - R_j^2\right)\right]^{\frac{n-1}{2}} \tag{6}$$

There are several algorithms that enable optimal choice of the *g* hyperparameter (see Ley and Steel, 2007; Steel, 2017, for a survey), but I will use two types of *g-prior*. The first one is the Unit Information Prior (UIP), where *g* is set according to a formula:

$$g = NT \tag{7}$$

where N is the number of observations included in the analysis. The second type of the *g-prior* is the risk inflation criterion Prior (RIC), proposed by Foster and George (1994), where g is set according to a formula:

$$g = K^2 \tag{8}$$

Here K is the maximum number of potential variables that can be included in the analysis.

The above mentioned *g-priors* are the most popular settings found in the literature. I have used them in order to verify the robustness of my results. If $NT > K^2$ then the RIC criterion can be used to create a "conservative" scenario, where there is a stronger prior assumption that β_j coefficients are close to 0.

2.2.2 Panel data with a lagged dependent variable

It should be noted that the fixed effect estimator is not well suited to dynamic models, which include lagged dependent variable in the set of regressors due to reasons discussed by Nickell (1981). To address this problem, for dynamic models I use correlated random effects (CRE) method developed in Alvarez and Arellano (2003) and applied in the BMA context by Moral-Benito (2012) and Moral-Benito and Roehn (2016). Let me briefly discuss the idea behind the CRE method. Suppose that I estimate model with (time-invariant) country-specific effects (μ_i) and a lagged dependent value (y_{t-1}):

$$y_{i,t} = \alpha y_{i,t-1} + x_{i,t}^T \beta + \mu_i + \varepsilon_{i,t} \tag{9}$$

where $x_{i,t}^T$ represents the matrix of explanatory variables. Following Moral-Benito and Roehn (2016), I take the following assumptions:

$$\varepsilon_{i,t} \mid y_i, x_i, \mu_i \sim N\left(0, \sigma_\varepsilon^2\right) \tag{10}$$

$$\mu_i \mid y_i, x_i \sim N\left(\phi \bar{y}_i + \delta \bar{x}_i, \sigma_\mu^2\right) \tag{11}$$

where y_i and x_i are vectors and matrices of observations for $y_{i,t}$ and $x_{i,t}$ and $\bar{y}_i$ and $\bar{x}_i$ are sample means. Model (9) can be rearranged into:

$$y_{i,t} = \omega_{i,t} \theta + \lambda_i + \varepsilon_{i,t} \tag{12}$$

where $\omega_{i,t} = \left(y_{i,t-1} - \overline{y}_i, x_{i,t} - \overline{x}_i, \overline{y}_i, \overline{x}_i\right)$, $\lambda_i = \mu_i - \phi\overline{y}_i - \delta\overline{x}_i$ and $\theta = \left(\alpha, \beta, \phi + \alpha, \delta + \beta\right)^T$. The resulting log-likelihood function is:

$$l\left(y_i|\omega_i\right) \propto -\frac{N}{2}log\overline{\sigma}_\varepsilon^2 - \frac{1}{2\overline{\sigma}_\varepsilon^2}\sum_{i=1}^{N}p\left(\overline{y}_i - \overline{\omega}_i^T\theta\right)^2 - \frac{N\left(T-1\right)}{2}log\sigma_\varepsilon^2 - \frac{1}{2\overline{\sigma}_\varepsilon^2}\sum_{i=1}^{N}\left(y_i^* - \alpha y_{i,(-1)}^* - x_i^*\beta\right)^T\left(y_i^* - \alpha y_{i,(-1)}^* - x_i^*\beta\right) \tag{13}$$

In the equations above, the $\overline{\sigma}_\varepsilon^2 = \overline{\sigma}_\lambda^2 + \frac{\overline{\sigma}_\varepsilon^2}{T}, \overline{\sigma}_\lambda^2 = var\left(\lambda_i\right)$, whereas $y_i^*, y_{i,(-1)}^*$ and x_i^* denote the orthogonal deviations of $y_i, y_{i,(-1)}$ (i.e. the lagged dependent variable) and x_i respectively. This function is maximised to get parameter estimates.

2.3 Assumptions related to the prior size of the model

The second important decision within the BMA framework relates to the choice of the model prior probability $P(M_j)$. The most intuitive choice would be to assume that each variable is independently included in the model with probability θ and is omitted with probability $1 - \theta$. Under such an assumption, the prior probability of M_j is given by Binomial distribution and depends on the number of regressors included in the model (K_j):

$$P\left(M_j\right) = \theta^{K_j}\left(1-\theta\right)^{K-K_j} \tag{14}$$

It should be noted that for a given θ the expected model size is θK and therefore if I want the expected model size to be K^*, then I need to fix the inclusion probability at:

$$\theta = \frac{K^*}{K} \tag{15}$$

Another possible approach is to assume that θ is a random variable and is drawn from a Beta distribution (binomial-beta prior, see Ley and Steel 2007):

$$\theta \sim Beta\left(a, b\right) \tag{16}$$

This change allows for reducing the impact of prior assumptions regarding the expected model size on the posterior probabilities $P(M_j|y)$. The reason is that the prior probability of models with a different number of regressors becomes flatter in comparison to the situation in which one would take the fixed value of θ. Furthermore, if $a = 1$ and $b = 1$, then one gets a (discrete) uniform prior probability for each model size, which minimises the influence of prior assumptions on the results.

2.4 Interpretation of the BMA analysis results

The posterior probability of the model allows a researcher to calculate the posterior probability inclusion (PIP) of each variable by summing the posterior probabilities of models that contain the analysed variable among regressors. Although PIP has a straightforward interpretation, there exists an alternative method to establish whether a given variable has an impact on the dependent variable. It exploits Bayesian approach to hypotheses testing, based on the Bayes factor (BF):

$$BF_{i,j} = \frac{p\left(Y|M_i\right)}{p\left(Y|M_j\right)} \tag{17}$$

where $p(Y|M_i)$ is the marginal likelihood of the model i. Bayes factors are used to compare model i to model j and values above 1 indicate that model i performs better. In the BMA context, I view the model i as the average marginal likelihood of a model containing analysed variable (opposed to average marginal likelihood of a model j without). For example, $BF = 4$ would mean that a model with the analysed variable is 4 times as likely as without (i.e. the posterior inclusion probability is equal to 80 %).[2]

Table 1 shows the most popular interpretations of the Bayes factor used in the Bayesian econometric literature and their posterior inclusion probability equivalents. On this basis, I propose to use the 95 % as the reference value for the analysis. A similar approach was also used by Moral-Benito and Roehn (2016).

2 It can be easily calculated as $\frac{4}{4+1}$.

Table 1. Interpretation of the Bayes factor

Bayes factor	*PIP equivalent*	*Evidence against H0*
	Jeffreys (1961)	
1 to 3.2	50.0 % to 76.2 %	Weak
3.2 to 10	76.2 % to 90.9 %	Substantial
10 to 100	90.9 % to 99.0 %	Strong
>100	>99.0 %	Decisive
	Kass and Raftery (1995)	
1 to 3	50.0 % to 75.0 %	Weak
3 to 20	75.0 % to 95.2 %	Positive
20 to 150	95.2 % to 99.3 %	Strong
>150	>99.3 %	Very Strong

Source: own elaboration based on *Jeffreys* (1961) and Kass and Raftery (1995).

The results obtained in the BMA analysis can also be visualised on a graph. Popular packages in R that offer BMA analysis have developed various ways of presenting the results. For instance, Figure 1 shows a graph summarising the result obtained in the "BMS" package developed by Zeugner and Feldkircher (2015). The figure shows only the top 500 models (i.e. with the highest posterior probabilities) cover approximately 99 % of the posterior probability space. The X-axis shows each model sorted by their posterior probability in decreasing order. The dashed lines separate one model from another, and in the case of Figure 1 one can observe that the first model has a posterior probability equal to 32 %. The Y-axis denotes the variables sorted by their posterior inclusion probability in decreasing order. The inclusion of the variables in the model is presented using light or dark gray colour. The light gray colour denotes negative sign, and the dark gray one denotes the positive sign of the variable in a given model. In the case of Figure 1, the variables "v1," "v2" and "v11" have the highest inclusion probabilities, because there are no white spaces on the graph. In general, the more "white spaces," the less likely is the variable to be a critical determinant of the analysed variable. Moreover, "v12" and "v9" variables change their colour, indicating that they have different signs in various models. Such a result also indicates that those variables are not likely to be an essential determinant of the analysed variable.

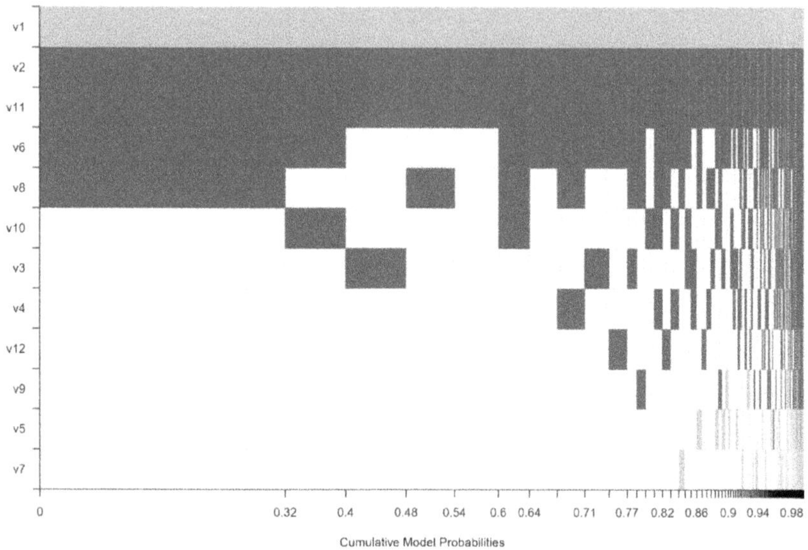

Figure 1. Visualisation of posterior inclusion probabilities: an example
Source: own elaboration.

Last but not least, the prior and posterior model size can also be visualised on a graph. For example, Figure 2 shows that the prior model size is uniformly distributed across the model space (see 2.3 for a reference), however, the mean posterior model size is almost 5, so in this case, one should expect that there are five determinants of the analysed variable.

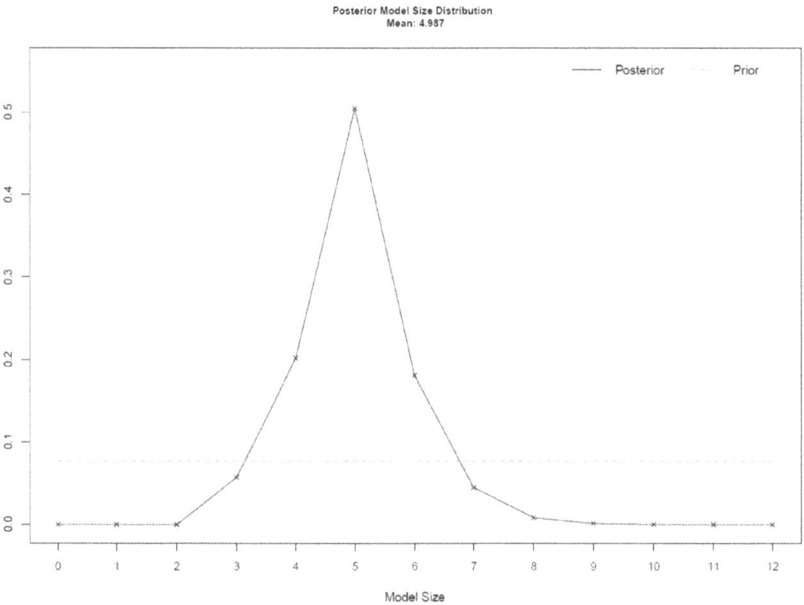

Figure 2. Visualisation of prior and posterior model size: an example
Source: own elaboration.

2.5 Dynamic Bayesian model averaging

Allowing the coefficients to differ in time is one of the most important extensions of the BMA framework. Such approach is called Dynamic (Bayesian) model averaging (DMA). I apply the DMA framework in chapter 5.6. Here I describe the details of this methodology. The analysed models are expressed as the dynamic linear processes (DLM) of the following form:

$$y_t = x_{i,t}^T \beta_{j,t} + \varepsilon_{j,t}, \varepsilon_{j,t} \sim N\left(0, V_j\right) \tag{18}$$

where the $x_{j,t}$ is the vector of predictors included in the model j and the is $\beta_{j,t}$ is the vector of time-varying coefficients evolving according to the formula:

$$\beta_{j,t} = \beta_{j,t-1} + \eta_{j,t}, \eta_{j,t} \sim N\left(0, W_{j,t}\right) \tag{19}$$

The changes of the coefficients values depend on the conditional variances: V_j from observational equation (18) and $W_{j,t}$ from the state equation (19). In the specific case that $W_{j,t} = 0$, the coefficients do not differ in time and one gets a static BMA algorithm. Testing all the possible combinations of $W_{j,t} = 0$ across j models is not possible, so the DMA framework introduces a forgetting factor, $0 < \delta \leq 1$, that allows controlling the magnitude of shocks to the coefficients by placing weights on the past observations. For example, $\delta = 0.99$ means that observations from 20 periods ago receive only 82 % of weight as the current observation, whereas $\delta = 0.9$ puts weight equal to 12 % for observations from 20 periods ago. As a result, the lower the δ, the greater the variability of the coefficients. In practice, the forgetting factor is estimated using recursive updating. The idea is to run the DMA algorithm over a grid of δ and then calculate the weighted average value of δ in time t on the basis of marginal likelihood of the models.

The next step of DMA is to compute the posterior probability of model j, $P(M_j|Y)$, i.e. the probability of the model conditional on the prior belief, $P(M_j)$, and the marginal likelihood of the model, $p(Y|M_j)$:

$$P\left(M_j|Y_t,Y_{t-1}\right)=\frac{p(Y|M_j,Y_{t-1})P\left(M_j|Y_{t-1}\right)}{\sum_{k=1}^{2^K}p(Y|M_k,Y_{t-1})P\left(M_k|Y_{t-1}\right)} \tag{20}$$

As compared to the static BMA approach, the difference lies in the fact that coefficients, models' posterior probabilities and variables' posterior inclusion probabilities can differ in time.

3 Current Account determinants[3]

There is a broad consensus among economists that unfavourable current account (CA) developments, through the accumulation of foreign financial assets and liabilities, had been one of the key drivers of the global financial crisis of 2008–2009 (Obstfeld and Rogoff, 2009; Blanchard and Milesi-Ferretti, 2010) and the European debt crisis (Alessandrini et al., 2014; EC, 2012; Chen et al., 2012; Ca' Zorzi and Rubaszek, 2012). Nowadays it is justified to argue that current account deficits and surpluses observed in the past in the euro area countries before the crisis were not "the end of Feldstein-Horioka puzzle," as described by Blanchard and Giavazzi (2002), but a sign of growing macroeconomic imbalances. This is reflected, among others, by including the CA to GDP ratio in the European Commission Macroeconomic Imbalance Procedure Scoreboard.

Even though there is a broad consensus on the importance of CA developments for macroeconomic stability, agreement is not reached in the discussion on what determines the external balance. On the one hand, the traditional, elasticity approach focuses predominantly on intratemporal factors such as relative demand and relative prices. On the other hand, the intertemporal approach emphasises the role of variables that affect decisions on investment and savings. The methods used to assess the dynamics of the current account are also diverse and range from econometric regressions (e.g. Chinn and Prasad, 2003) and "present value test" type of analysis (e.g. Sheffrin and Woo, 1990) to simulations with theoretical, general equilibrium models (see Singh, 2007, for a survey). This chapter contributes to the existing literature by applying panel regression techniques, and in particular Bayesian model averaging (BMA) methods, to verify whether intratemporal or intertemporal factors are most important in determining the current account.

---

3 This chapter is a version of a paper published as Dybka and Rubaszek (2017), co-authored by Michał Rubaszek

3.1 The economic theory

I begin with the definition and scope of the analysed variable. Current account is a part of the balance of payments of the economy that covers non-financial transactions that occur between the resident and non-resident entities. On the basis of the balance of payments manual developed by IMF (2013) (BOP6 methodology), current account can be divided into four main parts:

- Merchandise trade that includes exports and imports of goods. Those are recorded at the time when the change of ownership takes place.
- Services trade, which takes into account purchases and sales of services by residents, such as travel, transport, financial and other services. They are recorded on the basis of their actual delivery time.
- Primary income that covers earnings of employees working abroad for less than 12 months, paid by non-resident employers. Additionally, investment income from foreign financial assets such as dividends on equity, interest income from debt securities and loans is included. Retained profits in foreign companies are recorded proportionally to the ownership share of residents in those companies.
- Current transfers (secondary income) includes other resources provided or received by the residents without counterpart such as taxes, insurance premiums or money transfers made by workers staying abroad for over 12 months.

To illustrate the above, I will analyse the current account developments in Poland over the 2004–2019 period, presented in Figure 3. Poland had a current account deficit through the most of the analysed period, however, the deficits were gradually decreasing resulting in a minor surplus in 2017 and 2019. The reason for that change is that Poland started gradually offsetting the deficit in the merchandise trade with the exports of services (e.g. from shared services centres in Poland). On the other hand, the primary income account is gradually increasing the Polish current account deficit due to dividends and other income paid from foreign investments. The current transfers have less profound meaning for the current account developments.

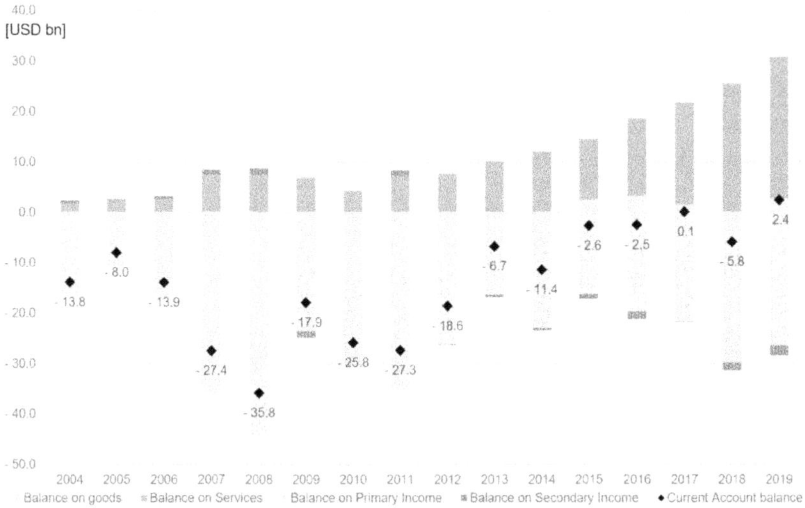

Figure 3. Current account developments in Poland
Source: own elaboration of data from Narodowy Bank Polski.

Current account changes can be analysed using many different techniques ranging from purely theoretical models such as intertemporal current account (ICA) models presented in Sachs (1981) or Obstfeld and Rogoff (1995) to various econometric regressions. First, I will briefly introduce the ICA framework. Following Ca' Zorzi and Rubaszek (2012), I assume that the representative household maximises its lifetime utility from consumption:

$$U_i = \sum_{i=0}^{\infty} \beta^i logC_{t+1} \tag{21}$$

subject to the intertemporal budget constraint:

$$B_t = R_t B_{t-1} + Y_t - C_t - I_t - G_t \tag{22}$$

and a transversality condition:

$$\lim_{n \to \infty} \beta^t U'(C_t) = 0 \tag{23}$$

All variables are expressed in per capita terms. U_t denotes the utility function of households, C_t private consumption, B_t stock of net foreign assets at the end of the period t, Y_t output, I_t investment and G_t government expenditure. The discount utility factor is equal to β. The current account is defined as the change in the stock of net foreign assets:

$$CA_t = B_{t+1} - B_t \tag{24}$$

After substituting equation (22) to equation (24) the current account is given as

$$CA_t = (R_t - 1)B_t + (Y_t - C_t - G_t - I_t) \tag{25}$$

The first part of equation (25) is related to the income balance and it shows that countries starting with a negative international position should save more in order to improve their balance (assuming that the current account deficit cannot be held infinitely). The second part of the equation, which can also be denoted as (S – I), i.e. savings minus investments, indicates that the crucial determinants of the current account are so-called intertemporal factors that affect the decision to save. Such factors include the general government budget balance and gross debt, total investment in the economy, domestic credit and foreign sources of financing (i.e. FDI inflows) and demographics (older societies tend to save less). It is also worth noting that in this framework the Ricardian equivalence does hold, meaning that the timing of taxes does not matter and the increase in consumption must be accompanied by an increase in future savings.

The outlined analysis can be further extended to account for additional factors. For example, Bussière et al. (2010), who focused on current account deficits in EU member states, modified the benchmark ICA model to include two additional effects – habit formation and liquidity constraints. In the traditional model individuals are characterised by their optimising behaviour with respect to intertemporal allocation of consumption, which means that Ricardian equivalence will hold. In the modified version there exists a proportion of agents (non-Ricardian) that consume all their income as they are not optimising. Fiscal surplus induces CA surplus as it lowers disposable income of non-Ricardian agents (they can spend less, as the Government collects more funds).

Even though the ICA model can be further extended, it usually takes into account limited number of factors. As a result, it is worth looking at the second strain of literature that uses econometric models to establish empirical links between current account and various potential determinants. For instance, Chinn and Prasad (2003) examined medium term determinants of CA imbalances using panel data regressions. Their research covered 89 countries, divided into industrial and developing countries (and sometimes regional differentiation was included). The authors begin with the cross-section analysis based on the full sample average (from 1971 to 1995) to establish which factors affect current account balances over long-term. They also apply panel estimates for 5 year non-overlapping averages of data. They include Least Squares regressions with time effects. The effects of public spending are significant only for developing countries. Additionally,fixed effects estimator was also used, but only as a way of checking the robustness of the results. The authors pointed out that according to cross-section results 40 per cent of variation is attributable to country-specific effects and hence wiping out the FE is not beneficial for understanding the cross-country differences.

Furthermore, it is also worth mentioning the Macroeconomic balances (MB) approach developed by Faruqee et al. (1999) and further extended by the IMF within the External Balance Assessment (EBA) framework in (Cubeddu et al., 2019), that focuses on the macroeconomic balance of the economy. In the Macroeconomic Balances approach there are two variables of interest: the real effective exchange rate (REER) and the current account balance. The key research question is evaluating at what level the current account would stabilise (CA^{norm}_t), assuming that the exchange rate remains unchanged and the output gap was closed (i.e. the economy would be in the steady state). Following the EBA approach one can express the current account norm as:

$$CA_t^{norm} = \alpha + \beta_1 cycl_t + \beta_2 mf_t + \beta_3 struc_t + \beta_4 policy_t \tag{26}$$

where $cycl_t$ includes cyclical factors such as the output gap and terms of trade, the mf_t denotes the macroeconomic fundamentals such as the net foreign assets, output per worker, GDP growth and reserve currency status (share of a country's currency in world reserve holdings), the $struc_t$ includes structural fundamentals related to demographics, institutional quality and natural resources exports and $policy_t$ denotes policy variables such as fiscal policy variables, health expenditure, foreign exchange interventions and financial excesses (a variable measuring the "excess" credit to GDP ratio compared to a long-term estimated trend).

As regards current account regressions within the Bayesian model averaging framework, it was introduced to the current account literature by Ca'Zorzi et al. (2012). In particular they used Bayesian Averaging of Classical Estimates (BACE) methodology proposed by Sala-I-Martin et al. (2004) to estimate the static relationship between the current account and 13 regressors. Their database included a balanced panel for 77 countries and 25 years of annual data, which were divided into two non-overlapping 12-year averages. The next milestone in the application of BMA methodology to analyse the current account was the study of Moral-Benito and Roehn (2016). The authors investigated current account developments with the use of a BMA method proposed by Moral-Benito (2012), which enables the inclusion of the lagged dependent variable in the set of regressors. Yet, in this study the dataset was relatively scarce and covered only 31 countries and 30 years of annual data divided into three non-overlapping 10-year averages.

The contribution of this chapter is threefold. First, I have created a relatively large, balanced panel dataset that covers 101 countries over 15 years. Second, I did not use averages over several years to balance the dataset that enabled me to provide results at higher frequencies. Third, research question is novel as I focus on the comparison of the relative importance of intra- and inter-temporal factors for the current account fluctuations.

3.2 Variable description

Below I outline the list of potential current account determinants along with a brief discussion on their theoretical expected signs:
Intratemporal factors

- **Real GDP growth.** Increasing demand should lead to higher imports and CA deterioration. Expected sign: negative.
- **Real effective exchange rate (REER).** Appreciation of domestic currency deteriorates price and cost competitiveness, which leads to CA

deterioration unless Marshall-Lerner condition does not hold. Expected sign: negative.

- **Net foreign assets to GDP ratio.** An increase in net foreign assets improves primary income balance, hence also the CA balance. Expected sign: positive. It should be noted, however, that apart from the direct effect, there is also indirect effect. High debt needs to be re-payed, which requires trade balance improvement. The adjustment process requires real exchange rate depreciation.
- **Fuel balance to GDP ratio.** Because of the direct effect on the trade balance, the expected sign is positive.

Intertemporal factors

- **Gross fixed investment to GDP ratio.** If foreign funds are used to finance domestic investment then high expenditures should result in a CA balance decline. Expected sign: negative.
- **Domestic credit provided by financial institutions to GDP ratio.** Financing the debt might require borrowing funds from abroad, hence the worsening of the current account balance. Expected sign: negative.
- **Foreign direct investment inflows to GDP ratio.** The inflow of long-term investment can affect the current account through higher imports (short horizon) and by generating outflows of cash related to paying dividends (longer horizon). Expected sign: negative.
- **General government budget balance to GDP ratio.** The twin deficits hypothesis indicates that the government budget balance is positively correlated with the CA balance. Expected sign: positive.
- **General government gross debt to GDP ratio.** A higher level of debt might discourage foreign investors leading to capital outflows and current account improvement. Expected sign: positive.
- **Relative per capita income,** adjusted by purchasing power parity. According to the permanent income hypothesis, the process of catching up is accompanied by temporarily lower savings, hence lower-income economies should have larger current account deficits. Expected sign: positive.
- **Population growth.** Higher population growth can be associated with immigrant inflow and relatively young population and both groups usually do not save much. Expected sign: negative.

- **Young (old) dependency ratio,** defined as the ratio of people under 15 (over 64) years old to the size of the labour force. A higher share of economic dependants in the population is associated with lower national savings. Expected sign: negative.

Other factors

- **Trade openness,** measured as the ratio of the sum of exports and imports to GDP and interpreted as a proxy for potential barriers to trade. Expected sign: ambiguous.
- **Voice and accountability, regulatory quality, rule of law and political stability.** The quality of institutions improves investors' trust, which enables borrowing more funds from abroad and running worse current account balance.

Expected signs: negative.

3.3 The data

For the purposes of the analysis, I have created a database covering 101 countries over years 2000–2014, using the following sources (see Table 2):

- IMF, World Economic Outlook (April 2016 edition, WEO)
- World Bank, World Development Indicators (WDI)
- World Trade Organization (WTO)
- Bruegel database on Real effective exchange rates (Bruegel)
- Worldwide Governance Indicators (WGI).

Table 2. Definitions of variables used in the analysis

Variable	*Description*	*Source*
Current account balance	Current account balance to GDP ratio	WEO
Total investment	Gross fixed investment to GDP ratio	WEO
General gov't balance	General government (GG) balance to GDP ratio	WEO
Fuel balance	Net trade of fuels to GDP ratio	WTO/WEO
Domestic credit	Domestic credit to GDP ratio	WDI
Trade openness	Sum of Exports and Imports to GDP ratio	WDI
GDP per capita (PPP)	Relative per capita income (PPP)	WEO
FDI inflows	Foreign direct investment to GDP ratio	WDI
General gov't gross debt	General government (GG) gross debt to GDP ratio	WEO
Voice and accountability	Voice and accountability indicator	WGI
Regulatory quality	Regulatory quality indicator	WGI
Population growth	Population growth	WEO
Rule of law	Rule of law indicator	WGI
Net foreign assets	Net foreign assets value to GDP ratio	WDI
Age dep. ratio, young	Age dependency ratio, young	WDI
Age dep. ratio, old	Age dependency ratio, old	WDI
REER	Real effective exchange rate	Bruegel
Political stability	Political stability indicator	WGI
Real GDP growth	Real GDP growth	WEO

Source: own elaboration.

In some cases, I have used data from Eurostat or local statistical offices, to fill in missing observations. Table 3 provides summary statistics for the data used in the analysis. One can observe that, on average, the analysed countries run a minor current account deficit, which is mainly related to the fact that there is a substantial number of developing countries included in the sample. Moreover, the minimum and maximum values of the current account seem to be quite surprising, but they were observed in Azerbaijan and Kuwait – counties that rely on oil exports and are vulnerable to oil price shocks. In general, the minimal and maximal values might seem to be quite extreme, but they stem from the wide spectrum of the countries included in the analysis (especially in the case of developing countries).

Table 3. Statistical summary of the data used in this chapter

	Min	*Max*	*Mean*	*Std. deviation*
Current account balance	-29.8	45.2	-1.3	8.9
Real GDP growth	-15.1	34.5	3.8	4.0
REER	55.8	234.5	100.4	13.3
Net foreign assets	-98.3	134.1	17.7	22.1
Fuel balance	-27.7	64.8	0.2	12.9
Total investment	6.6	58.0	23.7	6.5
FDI inflows	-16.1	87.4	4.3	5.8
General government balance	-32.2	43.3	-1.5	5.6
General government gross debt	1.6	249.1	49.3	32.1
Domestic credit	-70.4	380.3	72.5	64.9
GDP per capita (PPP)	437	92863	16875	16248
Age dep. ratio, young	15.5	107.2	46.5	23.1
Age dep. ratio, old	0.8	41.9	13.0	8.2
Population growth	-20.6	26.1	1.3	1.8
Trade openness	19.1	439.7	86.6	48.2
Regulatory quality	-1.5	2.2	0.3	0.8
Voice and accountability	-1.9	1.8	0.1	0.9
Rule of law	-1.9	2.1	0.1	1.0
Political stability	-2.8	1.7	-0.1	0.9

Source: own elaboration.

In the sensitivity analysis, I have divided the sample into two non-overlapping groups of developing and developed countries on the basis of World Bank Country and Lending Group classification.[4] I combined the countries classified by the World Bank as Low-income economies and Lower-middle-income economies into the developing countries group. The countries classified by the World Bank as the High-income economies and the Upper-middle-income economies were included in the developed countries group.

4 https://datahelpdesk.worldbank.org/knowledgebase/articles/906519-world-bank-countryand-lending-groups.

3.4 Baseline results

My baseline specification is the static model of the current account estimated with least squares (LS) estimator with a *Zellner's g-prior* selected on the basis of "Unit Information Prior" criterion (see chapter 2 for technical details). In the case of the prior model size, I assume binomial-beta prior that results in uniform prior probability for model size. The mean posterior model size is above 9 (see Figure 10).

Figure 5 provides a graphical visualisation of the obtained results. It shows that the first seven variables have posterior inclusion probability very close to 1. The following three variables also have a large PIP, although in some critical models those variables were not included.

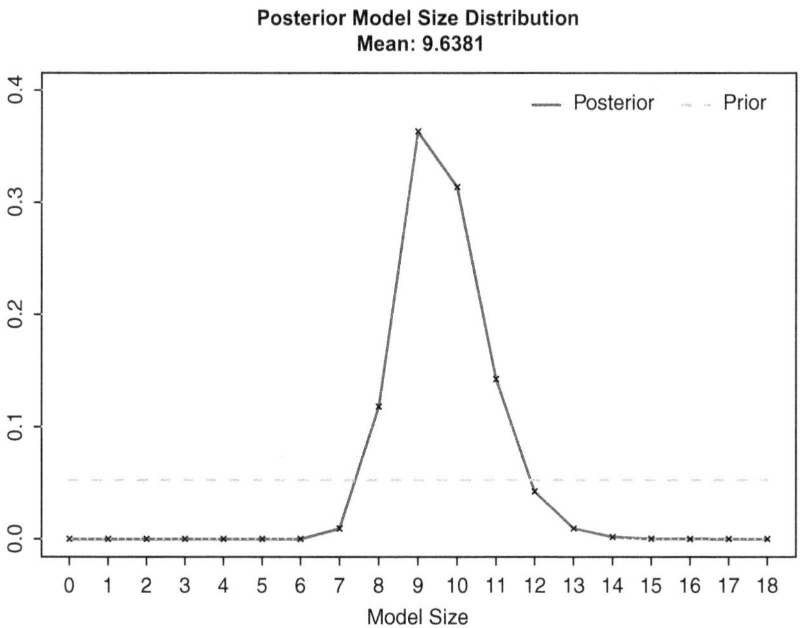

Figure 4. Posterior model size
Source: own elaboration.

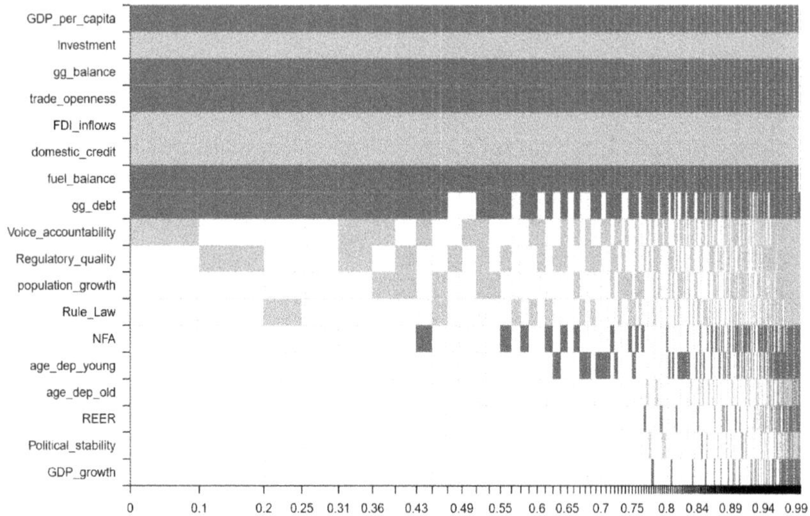

Figure 5. Variable selection
Source: own elaboration.

To get a more detailed view of the BMA analysis results I have also presented posterior inclusion probabilities and the weighted mean values of the coefficients obtained for the current account determinants in Table 4. To begin with, it seems very interesting and worthy to discuss that the intratemporal factors, except the fuel balance, proved to be of lower importance for the current account developments. In particular, the REER has an extremely low PIP. This result adds to the long-standing debate about the sources of international competitiveness of countries. For example, Kaldor (1978) showed that countries that experience REER appreciation also tend to increase their export market share, which suggests that there are other, structural factors that affect international competitiveness through their impact on the supply of export goods (a more detailed discussion is provided in chapter 4). In this sense, my findings confirm that REER cannot be regarded as the main driver of the external balance, and implicitly international competitiveness. I will further investigate this effect in chapter 4. Those results would question the usefulness of methods of calculating exchange rate misalignment on the basis of current account imbalances, as proposed by Williamson (1994) within the Fundamental Equilibrium Exchange Rate framework (see Ca' Zorzi et al.,

2020, for a detailed discussion). Moreover, the posterior inclusion probability (PIP) for Real GDP growth is very low and does not exceed 10 %, whereas the PIP for net foreign assets is below 20 %. Fuel balance[5]is the only intratemporal factor that proved to be important for current account developments, where the estimated parameter indicates that the pass-through from fuel balance to the current account is about 0.5, which means that an improvement in the fuel balance by 1 % of GDP increases the current account by about 0.5 % of GDP.

Table 4. Current account determinants: a baseline approach

	PIP	*Post. Mean*
	Intratemporal factors	
Real GDP growth	0.0371	0.0005
REER	0.0408	0.0002
Net foreign assets	0.1716	0.0028
Fuel balance	**1.0000**	**0.5426**
	Intertemporal factors	
Total investment	**1.0000**	**-0.5535**
FDI inflows	**1.0000**	**-0.1464**
General gov't balance	**1.0000**	**0.2663**
General gov't gross debt	0.8046	0.0143
Domestic credit	**1.0000**	**-0.0420**
GDP per capita (PPP)	**1.0000**	**0.0002**
Age dep. ratio, young	0.1368	0.0066
Age dep. ratio, old	0.0424	-0.0029
Population growth	0.2640	-0.0392
	Other factors	
Trade openness	**1.0000**	**0.0545**
Regulatory quality	0.4226	-0.5880
Voice and accountability	0.4500	-0.6735
Rule of law	0.2279	-0.3329
Political stability	0.0403	-0.0073

Notes: PIP and Post. mean denote posterior inclusion probability and posterior mean, respectively. The results for regressors with a strong impact on current account (PIP between 0.95 and 1.00) were bolded for convenience.

Source: own elaboration.

5 I have included various types of fuel that include: coal, oil and gas.

As regards intertemporal factors, the PIP for five of them amounts to 100 %.[6] Moreover, the estimated parameters are in line with expectations and of reasonable scale. An increase of investment by 1 % of GDP leads to current account decline by about 0.55 % of GDP. However, if this investment is in the form of FDI, the deterioration is larger by additional 0.15 % of GDP. A higher government deficit is also correlated with the current account, where the pass-through coefficient is about 0.25. The remaining two variables with PIP equal to unity are describing domestic credit expansion and the stage of economic development, as measured by GDP per capita.

For other factors, it was found that trade openness is an important determinant of the current account, whereas the indicators describing the quality of institutions were found to be of lower importance.

3.5 Sensitivity analysis

In this section I describe whether the results are sensitive to changes in the prior assumptions used in the BMA framework, changing the specification to dynamic form or division of the sample into groups of countries.

3.5.1 Sensitivity analysis with respect to prior assumptions

The first part of the sensitivity analysis was to check how stable are the baseline results with respect to the choice of models prior. For that purpose, I have created two scenarios. In the first scenario (named "conservative"), I choose such assumptions that make reaching the PIP threshold of 95 % is more difficult for each variable. I assume a fixed and low number of expected variables (three) to be included in the model and I also use the "risk inflation criterion" (RIC) for the choice of the optimal g-prior proposed by Foster and George (1994). Such criterion results in lower values of g-prior and thus strengthens the prior assumption that estimated coefficients are equal to 0. The second alternative set of assumptions is the "unconservative," where I assume a fixed and a high number of expected variables (number of variables available for selection minus three) to be included in the model.

6 I have collected the results only from the top 500 models that cover over 99 % of the total posterior probability space.

Table 5. Sensitivity of the results with respect to the prior assumptions

	CRE static model		*CRE dynamic model*	
	PIP	*Post. Mean*	*PIP*	*Post. Mean*
	Intratemporal factors			
Real GDP growth	0.0289	0.0004	0.0714	0.0004
REER	0.0949	0.0005	0.0448	-0.0001
Net foreign assets	**0.9994**	**0.0162**	**0.1786**	**-0.0019**
Fuel balance	**1.0000**	**0.5395**	**1.0000**	**0.4286**
	Intertemporal factors			
Total investment	**1.0000**	**-0.5568**	**1.0000**	**-0.4391**
FDI inflows	**1.0000**	**-0.1458**	**1.0000**	**-0.0901**
General gov't balance	**1.0000**	**0.2668**	**1.0000**	**0.1958**
General gov't gross debt	0.7746	0.0146	0.5403	0.0073
Domestic credit	**1.0000**	**-0.0410**	**0.9947**	**-0.0205**
GDP per capita (PPP)	**1.0000**	**0.2035**	**0.9965**	**0.1257**
Age dep. ratio, young	0.3561	0.0181	0.1697	0.0063
Age dep. ratio, old	0.0578	-0.0055	0.0862	0.0019
Population growth	0.3844	-0.0564	0.9090	-0.1625
	Other factors			
Trade openness	**1.0000**	**0.0543**	**1.0000**	**0.0326**
Regulatory quality	0.3478	-0.4730	0.1572	-0.1245
Voice and accountability	0.3861	-0.5795	0.4961	-0.6050
Rule of law	0.2517	-0.3718	0.1655	-0.1460
Political stability	0.2695	-0.0479	0.2933	-0.1770

Notes: PIP and Post. mean denote posterior inclusion probability and posterior mean, respectively. The results for regressors with a strong impact on current account (PIP between 0.95 and 1.00) were bolded for convenience.

Source: own elaboration.

The main conclusion of this exercise is that the choice of prior has not changed the estimates. I can observe only minor changes in the values of the PIP, which indicates that the results are robust with respect to different choices of prior assumptions on the model size and inclusion probability of the variables. In the unconservative scenario the PIPs are generally higher, but there is no new variable that exceeds the 95 % PIP threshold.

3.5.2 Dynamic model specification

In this part of the analysis, I estimate the models with correlated random effects (CRE) method on the basis of codes provided by Moral-Benito and Roehn (2016). The major advantage of the CRE estimator is that it allows for a dynamic specification without the Nickell (1981) bias. The time series for current account balance usually show high persistence and hence such dynamic specification seems to be worth considering. As regards model size prior, I use the same assumptions as in the baseline scenario (i.e. uniform distribution). I proceed in two steps.

First, I estimate a static model with a CRE estimator to verify if the change of estimation method leads to significant changes in the parameter estimates. In general, the same variables are identified as important in the BMA framework for both estimators, yet the only exception is the Net foreign assets, that has a very high PIP only in the case of the CRE estimates (see Table 6), but not in the case of LS estimator (see Table 4).

Second, I estimate the dynamic model with a lagged current account variable. On the one hand, the dynamic specification, compared to the baseline specification, does not lead to change in the set of identified crucial determinants of the current account (even though the PIP for the lagged current account balance amounting to 100 % indicates that dynamic specification is worth consideration). On the other hand, the Posterior Mean values of coefficients are generally lower (in absolute terms) in the CRE dynamic model specification in comparison to the baseline scenario and the only exception is the GDP per capita variable. This can be explained by the fact that short-term multipliers are lower than the long-term ones.

Table 6. Current account determinants: a correlated random effects (CRE) approach

	CRE static model		*CRE dynamic model*	
	PIP	*Post. Mean*	*PIP*	*Post. Mean*
Lagged Current account balance			1.0000	0.3728
	Intratemporal factors			
Real GDP growth	0.0289	0.0004	0.0714	0.0004
REER	0.0949	0.0005	0.0448	-0.0001
Net foreign assets	**0.9994**	**0.0162**	0.1786	-0.0019
Fuel balance	**1.0000**	**0.5395**	1.0000	0.4286
	Intertemporal factors			
Total investment	**1.0000**	**-0.5568**	**1.0000**	**-0.4391**
FDI inflows	**1.0000**	**-0.1458**	**1.0000**	**-0.0901**
General gov't balance	**1.0000**	**0.2668**	**1.0000**	**0.1958**
General gov't gross debt	0.7746	0.0146	0.5403	0.0073
Domestic credit	**1.0000**	**-0.0410**	**0.9947**	**-0.0205**
GDP per capita (PPP)	**1.0000**	**0.2035**	**0.9965**	**0.1257**
Age dep. ratio, young	0.3561	0.0181	0.1697	0.0063
Age dep. ratio, old	0.0578	-0.0055	0.0862	0.0019
Population growth	0.3844	-0.0564	0.9090	-0.1625
	Other factors			
Trade openness	**1.0000**	**0.0543**	**1.0000**	**0.0326**
Regulatory quality	0.3478	-0.4730	0.1572	-0.1245
Voice and accountability	0.3861	-0.5795	0.4961	-0.6050
Rule of law	0.2517	-0.3718	0.1655	-0.1460
Political stability	0.2695	-0.0479	0.2933	-0.1770

Notes: PIP and Post. mean denote posterior inclusion probability and posterior mean, respectively. The results for regressors with a strong impact on the current account (PIP between 0.95 and 1.00) were bolded for convenience.

Source: own elaboration.

3.5.3 Result for various groups of countries

In the third part of the sensitivity analysis I divide the sample into two subgroups of countries (developed and developing) to check whether the results are stable across the sample.[7] The first subgroup represents countries with higher income (65 countries, left column in Table 7) and the second subgroup includes lower income countries (36 countries, right column in Table 7).

Table 7. Current account determinants by subgroups of countries: a dynamic correlated random effects (CRE) model

	Higher income countries		*Lower income countries*	
	PIP	*Post. Mean*	*PIP*	*Post. Mean*
Lagged CA balance	**1.0000**	**0.3172**	**1.0000**	**0.3803**
	Intratemporal factors			
Real GDP growth	0.8547	-0.0023	0.0464	0.0010
REER	0.0688	-0.0007	0.0682	0.0003
Net foreign assets	0.2250	-0.0033	**0.9979**	**0.1208**
Fuel balance	**1.0000**	**0.5540**	0.2760	0.0306
	Intertemporal factors			
Total investment	**1.0000**	**-0.5799**	**1.0000**	**-0.2578**
FDI inflows	0.5794	-0.0293	**1.0000**	**-0.3280**
General gov't balance	**1.0000**	**0.1959**	**1.0000**	**0.1613**
General gov't gross debt	0.0381	-0.0002	0.8159	0.0205
Domestic credit	**0.9889**	**-0.0165**	0.5810	-0.0267
GDP per capita (PPP)	**1.0000**	**0.1426**	0.0625	0.0128
Age dep. ratio, young	0.0414	-0.0006	0.6926	0.0845
Age dep. ratio, old	0.0577	0.0011	0.0714	0.0266
Population growth	**0.9968**	**-0.2071**	0.0776	-0.0085
	Other factors			
Trade openness	0.8633	0.0199	0.8874	0.0320
Regulatory quality	0.0515	-0.0159	0.3172	-0.4468
Voice and accountability	0.4166	-0.5063	0.0844	0.0053
Rule of law	0.0798	-0.0074	0.5200	-0.9591
Political stability	0.1360	-0.0090	0.4691	-0.4881

Notes: PIP and Post. mean denote posterior inclusion probability and posterior mean, respectively. The results for regressors with a strong impact on current account (PIP between 0.95 and 1.00) were bolded for convenience.

Source: own elaboration.

7 The subgroups are not overlapping.

In both cases, I use the CRE method with lagged dependent variable, because the results of chapter 3.5.2 indicate that such variable should also be included, and it does not change significantly the resulting PIPs compared to the baseline scenario. The comparison of both columns in Table 7 leads to several interesting conclusions. First, the better access of developed countries to international financial markets enables them for easier external financing of investment spending, government expenditures or spending on fuel and other commodities. This is reflected in higher estimates for pass-through of the current account with respect to the above variables in the case of developed economies. On the other hand, the relationship between the current account and FDI inflows is much stronger for the group of developing countries, which can be explained by good access of foreign companies to external financing Kolasa et al. (2010).

Second, although the variables describing the quality of institutions (rule of law and political stability) have PIPs below the 95 % threshold, it seems that institutions are more important for developing countries than for developed ones. It is worth noting that in developing countries good institutions enable to maintain lower current account balance (i.e. run higher deficit). The reason is that good institutions reduce political risk of investing in a given economy for foreign companies. It seems that this risk is negligible for a group of developed countries.

Third, one can also observe that demographics (population growth) might also play an important role in shaping the current account balance in the case of the developed countries, but not for the developing ones. The negative sign might be related to the fact the in the developed economies, population growth often stems from the immigrant inflows, who often send part of their funds to the home country thus affecting the current account balance negatively.

Fourth, for both groups of countries the inertia of the current account turned out to be significant. However, the estimate of the autoregressive parameter, albeit comparable, is somewhat higher for developing countries. To conclude, the results in Table 7 show that the impact of macro-variables on the current account determinants might be heterogeneous among developed and developing countries.

3.6 Conclusions

In this chapter, I have studied various potential determinants of the current account. For that purpose, I have created a large balanced dataset for 101 countries over the period 2000–2014 and estimated a set of static and dynamic panels using BMA techniques. The comparison of the least squares (LS) and correlated random effects (CRE) estimates indicates that they produce very similar results, although the CRE method allows for the inclusion of the lagged dependent variable and keep the estimator unbiased.

The key results is that intertemporal factors, such as the investment rate, budget balance or relative stage of development can be viewed as the most important drivers of the current account. On the other hand, intratemporal factors seem to have lesser effect on the current account. The fuel balance is the only variable in this group that had posterior inclusion probability above the 95 % threshold. Those results are robust with respect to the prior assumptions in the BMA framework. As a result, I conclude that the intertemporal factors are more important determinants of the current account changes.

Another important conclusion from my study is that there are differences between developing and developed countries in terms of what drives the current account. High-income countries can easier finance investment and government expenditures with external resources as they have better access to international financial markets. This partly explains the paradox described by Lucas (1990), i.e. the capital can flow poor countries to rich ones. Next, for developing countries the quality of institutions was found to play a more pronounced role than in the case of developed countries. All in all, these results would indicate that the analysis of current account dynamics should take into account both systematic fundamentals – mostly intertemporal factors – as well as country specific developments.

4 Export market share determinants[8]

International trade has played an important role in the economy by "spreading the benefits of global integration and growth" (Krueger, 2006). It has therefore been the topic of numerous studies over decades. Krugman et al. (2012) even say that "the study of international trade and finance is where the discipline of economics as we know it began."

While the importance of export for growth is clear, there are some open questions regarding the key drivers of the export performance among countries. From the theoretical perspective, price factors such as the relative unit labour costs intuitively seem to be the major source of international competitiveness. However, Kaldor (1978) pointed to the fact that countries experiencing faster growth in relative unit labour costs and export prices had often outperformed other countries in terms of their export dynamics. This finding has sparked interest in non-price sources of international competitiveness. Fagerberg (1996) reports that such analyses were undertaken already in the late 1960s "following the advent of the neo-technological trade theories." Over time, with the increased availability of more detailed data, the literature evolved from analyses focusing on differences across countries (Magnier and Toujas-Bernate, 1994; Madsen, 2008) or sectors (Amable and Verspagen, 1995; Montobbio and Rampa, 2005) to firm-level investigations (for a review of firm-level studies see Dosi et al. 2015).

As regards the importance of institutions, it is well-established in the economic growth literature (North, 1989; Acemoglu et al., 2005; Rodrik, 2008). However, the question remains whether institutions are also important for international trade. Only a few recent studies look for sources of competitive advantage in institutional characteristics of exporting countries, and in particular the environment faced by exporters. Bournakis and Tsoukis (2016) and Bierut and Kuziemska-Pawlak (2017) provide evidence that price and non-price factors traditionally highlighted as important determinants of export performance, i.e. relative unit labour cost, R&D

8 This chapter is a version of a paper published as Bierut and Dybka (2021), co-authored by Beata Bierut.

expenditure as a share of GDP and patent applications per million population, maintain their significance. Both papers also document the significance of institutional factors (overall regulatory quality, barriers to entry, barriers to competition, barriers to FDI, quality of the legal system and protection of property rights) for export performance. Bournakis and Tsoukis (2016) also point to the importance of human capital and a non-linear, hump-shaped impact of government size (measured by tax receipts as a share of GDP) on export activity.

The lack of consensus on major determinants of export performance is the main motivation of this chapter, which claims to unify previous findings. My main contribution to existing literature involves the application of Bayesian model averaging, which (according to my best knowledge) has not been used in the context of export performance before. Instead of estimating just one model, I will test all possible combinations of models within the BMA framework, which means that my results will be robust with respect to variable selection uncertainty. To fully utilise the BMA approach, I have created a large database with various potential determinants of export performance identified on the basis of a literature review.

4.1 The economic theory

I will begin with the well-established gravity equation of international trade (see e.g. Fratianni, 2009; Krugman et al., 2012; Taglioni and Baldwin, 2014). Head and Mayer (2014) present the following simple general formulation of gravity equations:

$$X_{n,i} = G \times S_i \times M_n \times \phi_{n,i} \tag{27}$$

where $X_{n,i}$ denotes bilateral trade between exporter i and importer n, S_i measures "capabilities of exporter i as a supplier to all destinations," M_n captures "all characteristics of destination market n that promote imports from all sources," $\phi_{n,i}$ measures "bilateral accessibility of n to exporter i" and G denotes "gravitational constant." In the analysis of the overall performance of exporter i the whole world becomes the destination market n. In order to remove the need to specify the characteristics of the world demand for exports from country i, I will express the model in relative terms (see also e.g. Carlin et al., 2001; Bierut and Kuziemska-Pawlak, 2017):

$$\frac{X_{n,i}}{X_{n,B}} = \frac{G \times S_i \times M_n \times \phi_{n,i}}{G \times S_B \times M_n \times \phi_{n,B}} = \frac{S_i}{S_B} \times \frac{\phi_{n,i}}{\phi_{n,B}} \tag{28}$$

which implies that the trade performance of country *i* relative to benchmark region *B* (export market share, e.g. *B* = *EU* in Bierut and Kuziemska-Pawlak 2017) depends on its relative export capabilities and relative ease of access to world markets. For the purposes of the empirical analysis I will decompose the relative export capabilities and relative ease of access to world markets into the following components:

$$S_i \times \phi_{n,i} = P_i \times T_i \times Y_i \times Z_{n,i} \tag{29}$$

where P_{i} – is a measure of cost/price competitiveness, T_i – denotes innovativeness/technological capability, Y_i – includes production potential, $Z_{n,i}$ – encompasses the quality of the institutional environment. Some measures of institutional environment can be seen as related to export capabilities (Z_i, e.g. measures of the flexibility oflabourand product markets), while others measure ease of access to world markets ($Z_{n,i}$, e.g. measures of trade openness of destination market *n* to exporter *i*).

Next, I will substitute 29 into 28 and take the logarithm to obtain the relative measures equation:

$$\log \frac{X_{n,i}}{X_{n,B}} = \log \frac{P_i \times T_i \times Y_i \times Z_{n,i}}{P_B \times T_B \times Y_B \times Z_{n,B}} \tag{30}$$

Let lowercase letters denote logarithm of a ratio of a country value to the benchmark region value of a given variable (e.g. $\log \frac{X_{n,i}}{X_{n,B}} = x_i$) to express the estimated model specification in the following – relative – form:

$$x_{i,t} = \alpha_i + \beta_1 p_{i,t} + \beta_2 t_{i,t} + \beta_3 y_{i,t} + \beta_4 z_{i,t} + \varepsilon_{i,t} \tag{31}$$

where $x_{i,t}$ denotes the export market share of country *i* in time *t* in the overall value of the 28 European Union member states exports (EU is the benchmark region), $p_{i,t}$ – a vector of relative cost/price competitiveness measures, $t_{i,t}$ – a vector of relative innovativeness/technological capability measures, $y_{i,t}$ – a vector of relative production potential measures, $z_{i,t}$ – a vector of the relative quality of the institutional environment measures, α_i – the individual constant and $\varepsilon_{i,t}$ – an error term. Those measures are explained in detail in Table 17.

Apart from its simplicity, such an empirical approach has two major advantages. The first one is essential: since the seminal model by David Ricardo (the concept of comparative advantage), the drivers of international trade are seen in relative, rather than absolute, terms (see e.g. Cieślik and Parteka, 2018). Falling unit labour costs or increasing patents can still lead to a worse export performance if other countries reduce their labour costs or increase their number of patents at a faster rate. The second one is technical: expressing the variables in relative form diminishes the collinearity problem that one can expect in models with a large number of explanatory variables. Additionally, expressing variables in relative terms also means that any impact a global shock may have on export performance cancels out; hence, the results are less influenced by global shocks.[9]

4.2 Variable description

The list of potential export market share determinants that I have used in my regressions, and their expected impact, is as follows:

- **Unit labour cost (ULC).** Increase in the production costs per unit of output reduces price competitiveness of exports. Expected sign: negative (see also: Amable and Verspagen, 1995; Carlin et al., 2001; Bournakis and Tsoukis, 2016).
- **Std. dev. of NEER.** High volatility of the value of the currency increases the volatility of export revenues (and potentially input costs) and hence makes it more difficult and risky to plan export production and sales, discouraging export activity. Expected sign: negative.
- **Potential GDP.** The increase in production capacities allows increasing exports. Expected sign: positive (see e.g. Bierut and Kuziemska-Pawlak, 2017).
- **Capital output ratio.** The more capital is available for production, the more productive can the economy be. Expected sign: positive (see e.g.: Madsen, 2008).

9 Although country-specific shocks remain the element of the error term.

- **FDI stock.** Larger accumulated FDI stock means that the country was successful in attracting additional – foreign – investment, which should increase production and technological potential of its economy, and therefore its exports. Expected sign: positive (see e.g. Magnier and Toujas-Bernate, 1994; Amable and Verspagen, 1995; Dosi et al., 2015).
- **R&D expenditure.** Increased investment in the development of new technologies should increase the technological competitiveness of exports. Expected sign: positive (see e.g. Magnier and Toujas-Bernate, 1994; Dosi et al., 2015; Bournakis and Tsoukis, 2016).
- **Patent applications.** Development of new technologies should increase the technological competitiveness and therefore the export capacity of the country. Expected sign: positive (see also: Amendola et al., 1993; Amable and Verspagen, 1995; Bierut and Kuziemska-Pawlak, 2017).
- **School life expectancy.** Higher human capital should boost productivity of the economy and thereby also exports. Expected sign: positive (see e.g. Carlin et al., 2001).
- **Population with tertiary education.** As in the case of school life expectancy, higher human capital should boost productivity of the economy and thereby also exports. Expected sign: positive (see e.g. Bournakis and Tsoukis, 2016).
- **Size of government.** This variable broadly measures the extent to which the government and politics affect economic processes. Significant interference of government in the economy can lead to market distortions and inefficient asset allocation and hence can negatively affect exports. Expected sign: positive (higher values mean more economic freedom; see also Bournakis and Tsoukis, 2016).
- **Legal system and property rights.** High-quality legal and judicial systems, as well as strong protection of (property) rights, decrease the operating risks for firms and can increase their exports. Expected sign: positive (see e.g. Ma et al., 2010).
- **Sound money.** This variable broadly measures the stability of the value of money and hence aids planning of production and sales, also for exports; moreover, it supports cost competitiveness and provides mechanisms to reduce the volatility of export revenues. Expected sign positive.

- **Freedom to trade internationally.** This freedom is the necessary condition for the existence of exports (see e.g. Cieślik and Hagemejer, 2011). Expected sign: positive.
- **Regulation.** Higher quality of regulation, i.e. lower restrictions on the functioning of market mechanisms, boosts economic activity, and potentially also exports. Expected sign: positive (see also: Crozet et al., 2016; Bierut and Kuziemska-Pawlak, 2017).

4.3 The data

To provide the highest possible coverage of various measures of economic and institutional development I have used data from several sources (see Table 17). In general, data for manufactures' exports and FDI comes from UNCTAD databases, whereas technological and macroeconomic variables come from Eurostat, AMECO and the World Bank. Institutional indices are obtained from the Fraser Institute's Economic Freedom of the World Index database. My dataset covers the period 1995–2017 for 28 European Union member countries.

Table 8. Definitions of variables used in the analysis

Variable	*Description*	*Source*
Total manufactures	Value of manufactured goods' exports in USD	UNCTAD
Labour-intensive and resource-intensive manufactures	Value of labour-intensive and resource-intensive manufactured goods' exports in USD	UNCTAD
Low-skill and technology-intensive manufactures	Value of low-skill and technology-intensive manufactured goods' exports in USD	UNCTAD
Medium-skill and technology-intensive manufactures	Value of medium-skill and technology-intensive manufactured goods' exports in USD	UNCTAD
High-skill and technology-intensive manufactures	Value of high-skill and technology-intensive manufactured goods' exports in USD	UNCTAD
ULC	Real unit labour cost	Eurostat
Capital output ratio	Net capital stock per unit of gross domestic product at constant prices (%)	AMECO

Table 8. Continued

Variable	*Description*	*Source*
Potential GDP	Potential gross domestic product	AMECO
R&D expenditure	Value of Research & Development intensity (% of GDP spent on R&D)	Eurostat
FDI stock	Foreign direct investment, stock (% of GDP)	UNCTAD
Patent applications	Number of patent applications to the European Patent Office (per million people)	Eurostat, EPO
Std. dev. of NEER	Standard deviation of nominal effective exchange rate	Eurostat
School life expectancy	School life expectancy (SLE) is the total number of years of schooling (primary to tertiary) that a child can expect to receive, assuming that the probability of his or her being enrolled in school at any particular future age is equal to the current enrolment ratio at that age.	World Bank
Population with tertiary education	Share of population with tertiary education (%)	Eurostat
Size of government	Institutional variable measuring the extent to which government is affecting the markets (it also includes the share of state-controlled enterprises)	Fraser Institute, EFW
Legal system and property rights	Institutional variable measuring the overall quality of the legal system and property rights protection	Fraser Institute, EFW
Sound money	Institutional variable measuring the extent of inflation control, restriction of foreign currency controls and other areas affecting the freedom within the monetary system	Fraser Institute, EFW
Freedom to trade internationally	Institutional variable measuring to what extent goods and services can be bought and sold across international borders with little or no government tariffs, quotas, prohibitions etc.	Fraser Institute, EFW
Regulation	Institutional variable measuring the regulatory interference in the markets	Fraser Institute, EFW

Notes: EFW – Economic Freedom of the World. EPO – European Patent Office.

Source: own elaboration.

The dynamics of the dependent variable is presented in Figure 6. It shows percentage point changes in export market shares for the EU countries between 1995 and 2017. Around half of the EU countries did not experience any substantial changes in their export positions over this period. However, some countries (notably New Member States (NMS) such as Poland, the Czech Republic and Hungary), substantially increased their export market shares. It seems noteworthy that in the case of the NMS countries export also significantly contributed to their GDP growth (see Hagemejer, 2018). On the other hand, other countries (the United Kingdom, France and Italy), saw a significant deterioration of their export position.

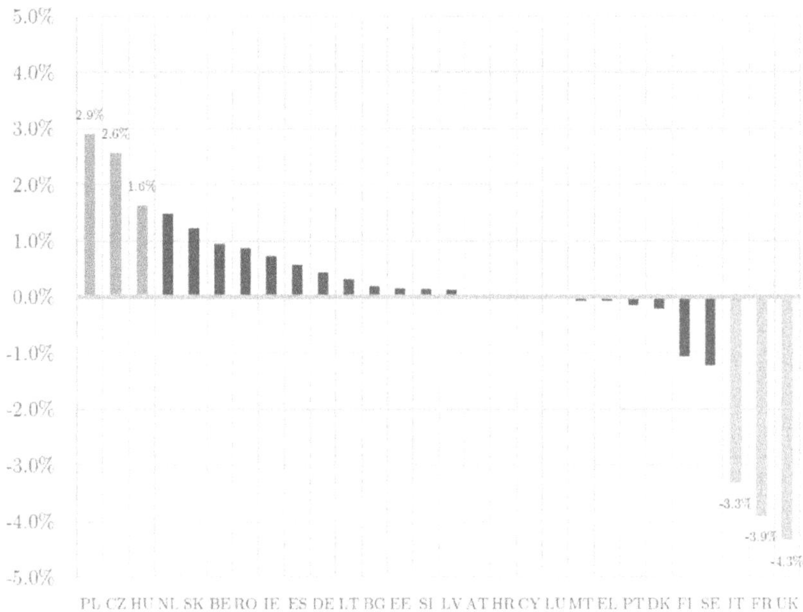

Figure 6. Changes in export market shares of the EU countries (1995–2017)
Source: own elaboration of Eurostat data.

Table 9 shows the summary statistics for the New Member States (i.e. countries that joined the EU in 2004, 2007 and 2011) divided into 1995–2003 period (prior to joining the EU) and the 2004–2017 period. The mean values of all variables considered in the analysis has improved after joining the EU. The largest changes can be observed in the case of sound money institutional index and the standard deviation of NEER (showing stabilisation of the monetary policy and the exchange rates), the Regulation institutional index as well as the potential GDP. On the other hand, ULC and the Capital output ratio observed only a minor change compared to the period before the EU accession.

Table 9. Statistical summary for EU New Member States

	1995-2003			*2004-2017*		
	Min	*Mean*	*Max*	*Min*	*Mean*	*Max*
ULC	0.38	0.52	0.68	0.37	0.50	0.62
Std. deviation of NEER	0.16	8.06	363.89	0.28	1.56	19.58
Capital output ratio	94.78	199.02	318.64	89.71	203.13	303.20
Potential GDP	4.6	66	309	6.5	85	453
R&D expenditure	0.20	0.66	1.49	0.34	0.91	2.58
FDI stock	2.18	23.70	71.32	19.41	195.59	1811.63
Patent applications	0.13	5.49	41.79	0.63	13.99	69.10
School life expectancy	10.37	13.40	16.59	13.41	15.39	17.64
Population with tertiary education	4.90	14.28	35.30	8.70	20.56	38.10
Size of government	1.75	5.11	6.94	4.40	6.37	7.79
Legal system and property rights	4.80	6.01	7.21	4.66	6.16	7.51
Freedom to trade internationally	5.88	7.76	9.73	7.20	8.01	8.68
Sound money	0.73	6.46	9.61	6.54	9.21	9.81
Regulation	3.75	6.28	7.69	6.29	7.46	8.44

Source: own elaboration

The Old Member States also improved their position in case of majority of the analysed variables over the recent years (see Table 10), with some institutional variables (freedom to trade internationally and Legals System and Property Rights) being the exception that have decreased their values. Such results indicate that institutions can be part of the explanation why New Member States improved their export market shares compared to the Old-EU. The improvement of the technological factors among the old members of the EU was also less profound than in the case of the NMS.

Table 10. Statistical summary for EU Old Member States

	1995-2003			*2004-2017*		
	Min	*Mean*	*Max*	*Min*	*Mean*	*Max*
ULC	0.44	0.56	0.64	0.34	0.55	0.61
Std. deviation of NEER	0.33	1.39	4.84	0.20	1.06	6.22
Capital output ratio	193.91	284.92	406.82	183.92	291.40	450.64
Potential GDP	27.6	741	2613	38.9	872	3135
R&D expenditure	0.42	1.72	3.91	0.53	1.99	3.75
FDI stock	5.58	42.05	207.04	9.09	68.35	376.18
Patent applications	1.40	117.57	277.19	5.60	151.87	348.84
School life expectancy	11.83	15.83	18.85	13.50	16.74	20.76
Population with tertiary education	6.00	18.16	27.50	10.00	26.22	40.40
Size of government	2.09	4.59	6.73	3.50	5.47	7.08
Legal system and property rights	5.67	7.64	9.01	5.34	7.58	9.14
Freedom to trade internationally	7.85	8.91	9.39	7.55	8.24	9.12
Sound money	7.34	9.54	9.84	7.98	9.55	9.86
Regulation	4.98	7.02	8.54	5.34	7.45	8.60

Source: own elaboration.

Figure 7 presents scatter plots of the selected variables. The x axes denote the level of the export market share regressor in 1995, and the y axes – the level in 2017. Countries depicted by the points lying above the 45-degree line experienced an improvement in the particular variable in 2017 compared to 1995. The charts show that the success of the countries that noticeably increased their export market shares was mainly associated with improvements in their institutional environment, in particular Regulation, sound money and size of government. Moreover, Poland, the Czech Republic and Hungary also improved their relative position in terms of patent applications. Positive changes in export performance observed in the New Member States (NMS) of the EU can also be related to enlargement of the EU and resulting opening of the EU markets for the NMS that to some extent is visible in the changes in freedom to trade internationally (such change can support gaining the export market share by intensive margins, i.e. better adaptation to the existing markets, see e.g. Gilbert and Muchová, 2018). The large deterioration in the export position of the United Kingdom, France and Italy also seems to have been mainly associated with relatively worse performance in patenting activity.

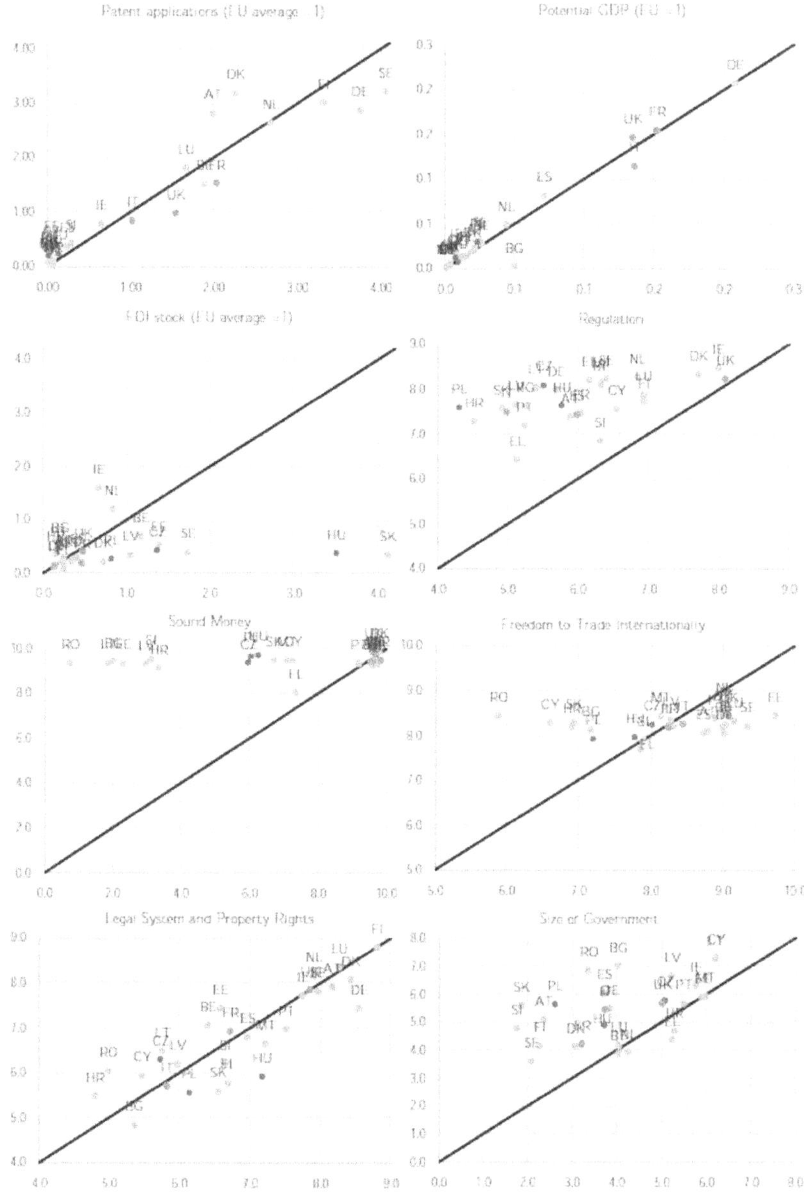

Figure 7. Development of selected export market share drivers in the EU countries (2017 versus 1995)
Source: own elaboration.

4.4 Baseline results

To construct the baseline scenario, I have used the Least Squares estimator with a *Zellner's g-prior* selected on the basis of "Unit Information Prior" criterion (see chapter 2.2.1 for a reference). Figure 8 shows that in my baseline scenario the prior model size is uniformly distributed across the model space (see chapter 2.3 for a reference). The mean posterior model size is almost nine, so up to nine variables could be identified as the key determinants of the export market share.

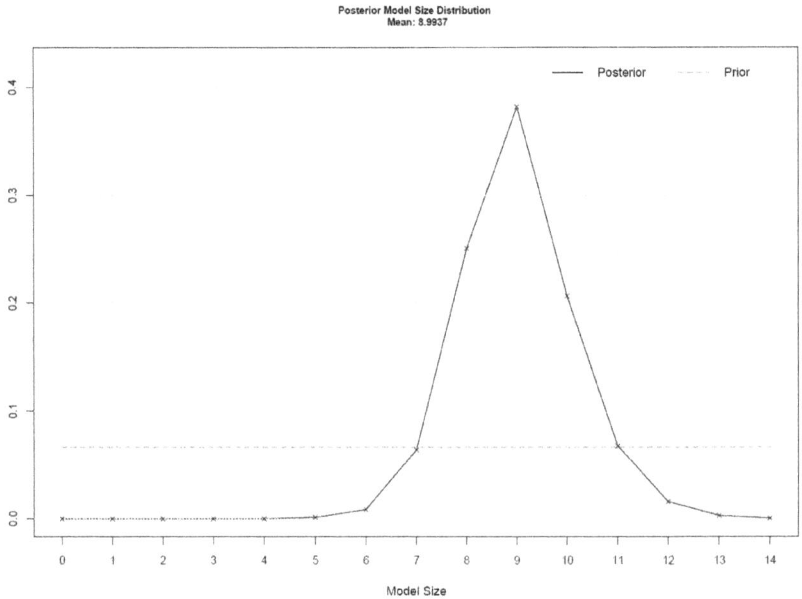

Figure 8. Posterior model size
Source: own elaboration.

Figure 9 provides a graphical visualisation of the obtained results. It shows that the first six variables have posterior inclusion probability very close to 1. The following three variables also have a large PIP, although some visible white spots are indicating that in some critical models those variables were not included.

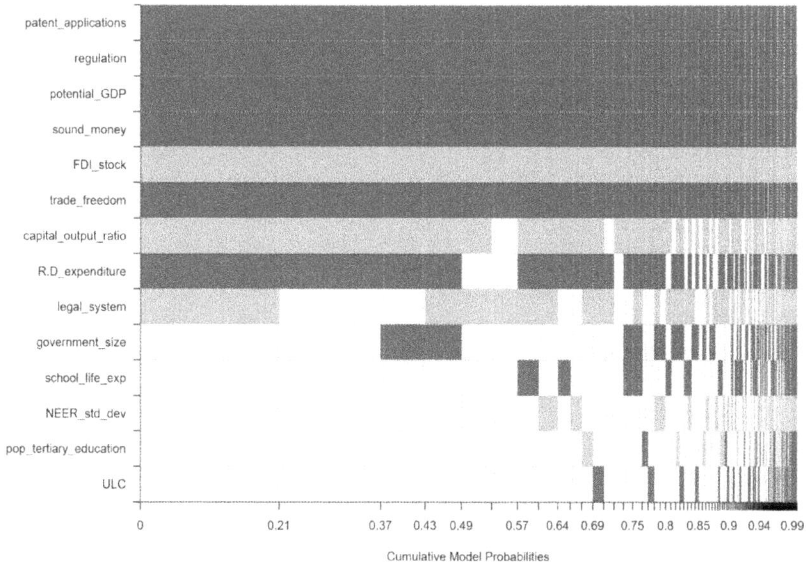

Figure 9. Visualisation of posterior inclusion probabilities
Source: own elaboration.

To get a more detailed view of the BMA analysis results I have also presented posterior inclusion probabilities and the weighted mean values of the coefficients obtained for the export market share for the total value of manufactured goods in Table 16. To get a better understanding technological and institutional factors effects on export market share, I also analyse the PIP and mean coefficient values obtained for different types of manufactured goods export market shares (see Table 12). Studying various types of manufactures allows me to study not only the direct effect on export market share (as in Table 16), but also a transformational impact – from less to more technologically advanced exports.

Table 11. Baseline results for total manufactures exports

	Total manufactures	
	PIP	*Post. mean*
Price Competitiveness		
Std. dev. of NEER	0.12	-0.002
ULC	0.08	0.002
Technological factors and human capital		
Patent applications	**1.00**	**0.245**
Potential GDP	**1.00**	**0.250**
FDI stock	**1.00**	**-0.090**
Capital output ratio	0.87	-0.290
R&D expenditure	0.82	0.111
School life expectancy	0.15	0.034
Population with tertiary education	0.08	0.000
Institutional factors		
Regulation	**1.00**	**0.864**
Sound money	**1.00**	**0.229**
Freedom to trade internationally	**0.99**	**0.920**
Legal system and property rights	0.62	-0.297
Size of government	0.26	0.033

Notes: PIP and Post. mean denote posterior inclusion probability and posterior mean, respectively. The results for regressors with a strong impact on exports (PIP between 0.95 and 1.00) were bolded for convenience.

Source: own elaboration.

The results indicate that price factors have a limited impact on the overall export performance of the EU countries, which confirms the results from the previous chapter. This can be due to the specific characteristics of the analysed group of countries. In the case of the Western European countries, low price sensitivity of exports is most likely related to their specialisation in high-tech exports (which is also confirmed by a highly significant impact of the technological factors on their export performance). In the case of the catching-up NMS countries, the results may be stemming from the paradox discussed in Kaldor (1978).

	LRI		LTI		MTI		HTI	
	PIP	*Post. mean*	*PIP*	*Post. mean*	*PIP*	*Post. mean*	*PIP*	*Post. mean*
Price competitiveness								
Std. deviation of NEER	0.12	-0.001	0.06	0.000	0.47	-0.016	0.16	-0.004
ULC	0.09	0.000	0.88	-0.692	0.14	0.031	0.09	0.013
Technological factors and human capital								
Patent applications	**1.00**	**0.201**	**1.00**	**0.216**	**1.00**	**0.306**	**1.00**	**0.283**
Potential GDP	0.09	0.000	**0.99**	**0.302**	**1.00**	**0.289**	**1.00**	**0.454**
FDI stock	**1.00**	**-0.204**	**1.00**	**0.130**	**1.00**	**-0.155**	**0.98**	**-0.099**
Capital output ratio	0.38	-0.087	0.06	0.000	0.08	-0.003	0.68	-0.275
R&D expenditure	**0.98**	**-0.192**	**0.97**	**0.272**	**0.97**	**0.197**	**1.00**	**0.358**
School life expectancy	0.60	-0.283	0.90	0.744	0.18	0.056	0.41	0.210
Population with tertiary education	**0.99**	**-0.246**	**0.97**	**-0.340**	0.09	0.004	0.31	0.049
Institutional factors								
Regulation	**1.00**	**1.074**	0.10	0.027	**1.00**	**1.217**	**1.00**	**1.021**
Sound money	**1.00**	**0.352**	0.06	0.000	**1.00**	**0.462**	0.10	0.005
Freedom to trade internationally	**1.00**	**-1.147**	0.06	-0.003	**1.00**	**1.615**	**1.00**	**2.190**
Legal system and Property rights	0.10	-0.013	0.47	-0.353	0.13	-0.035	0.73	-0.565
Size of government	**0.99**	**0.314**	0.20	-0.042	**0.99**	**0.366**	0.15	0.021

Notes: PIP and Post. mean denote posterior inclusion probability and posterior mean, respectively. The results for regressors with a strong impact on exports (PIP between 0.95 and 1.00) were bolded for convenience.
LRI – Labour-intensive and resource-intensive manufactures
LTI – Low-skill and technology-intensive manufactures
MTI – Medium-skill and technology-intensive manufactures
HTI – High-skill and technology-intensive manufactures

Source: own elaboration.

I have used both the data on the number of patent applications as well as research and development intensity (R&D expenditure expressed as % of GDP). Earlier literature often focused on either R&D expenditure (e.g. Magnier and Toujas-Bernate, 1994; Anderton, 1999) or number of patents (e.g. Amendola et al., 1993; Amable and Verspagen, 1995) and usually showed positive and statistically significant results. However, when both R&D intensity and patents were used the obtained results were less clear – Wakelin (1998) showed that both variables had a positive and statistically significant effect on export performance, whereas Carlin et al. (2001) reported that neither R&D expenditure nor the number of patents had a statistically significant impact. My results provide some insight into this discussion. In general, the measure of patent applications proves to be a better variable to analyse technological competitiveness as regards trade in manufactured goods, as its posterior inclusion probability (PIP) is equal to 1 (meaning that among the top 500 models, this variable was included in all the cases), whereas R&D expenditure has a lower PIP. At a first glance, such results can be viewed as evidence that R&D investment is more likely to be indirectly beneficial for export performance, i.e. when it is successful, resulting in a large number of patent applications (see also Bournakis, 2014, for a discussion on cross-industry knowledge spillovers). The results in Table 12 show that patent applications have a strong impact on all types of exports and that it increases with their technological intensity. As far as the R&D expenditure is concerned, its impact is negative in the case of labour-intensive and resource-intensive manufactures. However, the estimated effect for other types of manufactures is positive, confirming the R&D's transformational impact on exports: R&D expenditure appears to be rather used to specialise in the production and exports of more technologically advanced goods. As a result, the increase in R&D expenditure can be associated with the process of a technological upgrading of the manufactures, thus resulting in a decrease in the value of low skill and technology intensive exports.

In addition to technological factors, the potential GDP also has a strong positive impact on export performance. The strength of this effect increases with the level of technological intensity of exports, which indicates that higher potential GDP is often associated with more technology-intensive manufactures. The impact of the capital output ratio on exports is insignificant, while the impact of the FDI stock is significantly negative; its strength decreases with the technological intensity of exports. It, therefore, seems that the negative impact of FDI stock on exports stems from the type of FDI inflows into the EU countries (mainly into services and manufacturing) and their transformational impact on the production structure in host countries (away from agriculture, mining and quarrying and into manufacturing and services). Moreover, such result also points out that horizontal rather than vertical FDI inflows are more popular in the case of manufacturing. Vertical foreign direct investments means that the new establishment plays the role of a supplier in the production supply chain and therefore increases the value of exports. In the case of horizontal FDI an investor establishes the same type of business activity in a foreign country as it operates in its home country, which means that the resulting production is only crowding out the imports rather than stimulating exports. For a general discussion on the impact of FDI on home and host countries, see Lipsey (2002). The results regarding human capital show that it does not have a strong direct impact on export performance of the EU countries. However, it seems again to have an indirect impact, as a factor transforming their production and export structure. A higher share of population (and therefore labour force) with tertiary education appears to reduce exports of labour- and resource-intensive exports, while having no significant impact on exports of other types of manufactures. It therefore seems likely, that increases exports of services (see also Mulliqi et al., 2019). The school life expectancy does not seem to have a significant impact on the export performance.

The results from Table 16 and Table 12 show that institutional factors also play an important role in shaping the international export competitiveness. Similarly to some of the factors discussed above, institutions can affect the export performance in two ways: (i) directly stimulating exports or (ii) transforming export structures.

The regulatory environment belongs to the first category, as one can observe a significant positive impact of the quality of regulations on the export performance. sound money, which supports and preserves gains from trade, also appears to have a strong positive impact on exports. Although freedom to trade internationally has a significant positive impact on export performance, such impact can be misunderstood if looked only at the aggregated level. The details of the mechanism connecting freedom to trade internationally with export performance unravels when specific types of goods are considered. Freedom to trade internationally has a strong and negative impact on the labour-intensive and resource-intensive manufactures. This result stems from the fact that there is little room for differentiation in case of such goods. As a result, a lack of trade barriers (such as tariffs, quotas etc.) means that domestic producers of such goods face fierce competition from foreign producers, mostly focusing on price, thus decreasing their profit margins. This, in turn, provides incentives to move to more skill- and technology-intensive production. Indeed, my results present strong evidence that higher freedom to trade internationally stimulates exports of the medium and high-skill and technology-intensive manufactures. Such result is similar to Marjit and Ray (2017) who claim that in the presence of advanced technology, exports are augmented with the rise in competition. In the context of the EU, this result is also related to the emergence of the European supply chains and their impact on production and export structures in participating countries. It seems therefore that freedom to trade internationally can be associated with the transformation of the export structures: removing obstacles to trade pushes producers to specialise in more skill- and technology-intensive manufactures.

Contrary to my hypotheses, legal system and property rights as well as the size of government do not seem to strongly affect the overall value of exports. In the case of the latter category one can identify significant effect only in some types of manufactures.

4.5 Sensitivity analysis

In this section, I describe whether the results are sensitive to changes in the prior assumptions used in the BMA framework or more detailed specification of the institutional variables.

4.5.1 Sensitivity analysis with respect to prior assumptions

To verify the robustness of the results, I conduct the sensitivity analysis concerning the choice of the prior assumptions in the BMA framework. In the first alternative (named "conservative") I choose the most conservative set of prior assumptions, which means that reaching the PIP threshold of 95 % is more difficult for each variable. I assume a fixed and low number of expected variables (three) to be included in the model and I also use the "risk inflation criterion" (RIC) for the choice of the optimal *g-prior* proposed by

(Foster and George, 1994). Such criterion results in lower values of *g-prior* and thus strengthens the prior assumption that estimated coefficients are equal to 0. The second alternative set of assumptions is the "unconservative," where I assume a fixed and a high number of expected variables (number of variables available for selection minus three) to be included in the model.

The results presented in Table 13 show that my findings are largely robust to different prior assumptions used in the BMA. The same holds true for the results obtained for different categories of exports: they are also robust with respect to the prior assumptions in the BMA framework (see Tables 22–25 in the Appendix).

Table 13. Sensitivity analysis of baseline results for total manufactures' exports

	Baseline assumptions		*Conservative assumptions*		*Unconservative assumptions*	
	PIP	*Post. mean*	*PIP*	*Post. mean*	*PIP*	*Post. mean*
Price competitiveness						
Std. dev. of NEER	0.12	-0.002	0.04	-0.001	0.20	-0.002
ULC	0.08	0.002	0.02	0.001	0.13	0.003
Technological factors and human capital						
Patent applications	**1.00**	**0.245**	**1.00**	**0.249**	**1.00**	**0.243**
Potential GDP	**1.00**	**0.250**	**1.00**	**0.261**	**1.00**	**0.247**
FDI stock	**1.00**	**-0.090**	**0.99**	**-0.083**	**1.00**	**-0.092**
Capital output ratio	0.87	-0.290	0.66	-0.218	0.94	-0.309
R&D expenditure	0.82	0.111	0.53	0.072	0.92	0.126
School life expectancy	0.15	0.034	0.05	0.013	0.24	0.052
Population with tertiary education	0.08	0.000	0.02	0.001	0.13	0.000
Institutional factors						
Regulation	**1.00**	**0.864**	**1.00**	**0.863**	**1.00**	**0.863**
Sound money	**1.00**	**0.229**	**1.00**	**0.234**	**1.00**	**0.226**
Freedom to trade internationally	**0.99**	**0.920**	0.94	0.834	**1.00**	**0.944**
Legal system and property rights	0.62	-0.297	0.47	-0.256	0.72	-0.329
Size of government	0.26	0.033	0.10	0.013	0.38	0.047

Notes: PIP and Post. mean denote posterior inclusion probability and posterior mean, respectively. The results for regressors with a strong impact on exports (PIP between 0.95 and 1.00) were bolded for convenience.

Source: own elaboration.

4.5.2 Results on the basis of extended sets of regressors

In this section, I analyse more detailed sub-indices measuring different aspects of institutional quality from the Fraser Institute. At the same time, I drop the general institutional quality measures, as they are often (linear) combinations of the included sub-indices. The results presented in Table 14 and Table 15 show that including more detailed institutional sub-indices does not lead to significant changes in results obtained for price competitiveness, technological factors as well as human capital.

Table 14. Results for the extended set of regressors for total manufactures exports

	PIP	*Post. mean*
Price Competitiveness		
Std. dev. of NEER	0.07	0.013
ULC	0.04	0.000
Technological factors and human capital		
Patent applications	**1.00**	**0.231**
Potential GDP	**1.00**	**0.310**
FDI stock	0.73	-0.037
Capital output ratio	0.51	-0.129
R&D expenditure	0.08	0.005
School life expectancy	0.05	0.006
Population with tertiary education	0.05	-0.001
Institutional factors		
Regulatory trade barriers	1.00	0.939
Tariffs	1.00	0.803
Judicial independence	0.99	-0.265
Inflation: most recent year	0.95	0.202
Money growth	0.57	0.045
Government consumption	0.57	-0.055
Business regulations	0.56	0.180
Credit market regulations	0.51	0.088
Top marginal tax rate	0.46	0.032
Controls of the capital and people movement	0.14	-0.009
Standard deviation of inflation	0.11	0.010
Transfers and subsidies	0.11	0.008
Integrity of the legal system	0.08	-0.011
Impartial courts	0.07	-0.005

Table 14. Continued

	PIP	*Post. mean*
Protection of property rights	0.07	-0.008
Government enterprises and investment	0.04	-0.001

Source: own elaboration.

Table 15. Results for the extended set of regressors for different categories of exports

	LRI		*LTI*		*MTI*		*HTI*	
	PIP	*Post. mean*	*PIP*	*Post. mean*	*PIP*	*Post. mean*	*PIP*	*Post. mean*
Price competitiveness								
Std. deviation of NEER	0.05	-0.004	0.22	-0.123	0.48	0.254	0.48	0.254
ULC	0.06	-0.001	0.02	0.000	0.26	-0.008	0.04	0.000
Technological factors and human capital								
Patent applications	**1.00**	**0.192**	**1.00**	**0.217**	**1.00**	**0.299**	**1.00**	**0.267**
Potential GDP	0.05	0.001	**0.99**	**0.318**	**1.00**	**0.364**	**1.00**	**0.486**
FDI stock	**1.00**	**-0.161**	**0.98**	**0.159**	0.92	-0.067	0.28	-0.015
Capital output ratio	0.11	-0.019	0.03	0.004	0.03	0.001	0.81	-0.363
R&D expenditure	**1.00**	**-0.292**	0.54	0.114	0.11	0.010	**0.97**	**0.252**
School life expectancy	0.94	-0.643	0.91	0.917	0.04	0.006	0.07	0.020
Population with tertiary education	**0.99**	**-0.283**	0.34	-0.083	0.11	0.012	0.34	0.071
Institutional factors								
Regulatory trade barriers	**1.00**	**0.746**	0.06	0.016	**1.00**	**1.240**	**1.00**	**1.123**
Tariffs	0.06	-0.011	0.02	-0.001	**1.00**	**1.156**	**1.00**	**1.766**
Judicial independence	0.88	-0.201	0.04	0.005	0.47	-0.105	0.07	-0.010
Inflation: most recent year	**1.00**	**0.258**	0.04	0.004	**1.00**	**0.344**	0.10	0.013
Money growth	0.05	0.002	**0.99**	**0.510**	0.05	-0.003	**0.95**	**0.362**
Government consumption	**1.00**	**0.193**	0.11	0.009	0.06	0.002	0.06	0.003
Business regulations	0.05	0.002	0.05	-0.003	0.12	-0.009	0.31	-0.035
Credit market regulations	**0.99**	**0.530**	0.06	0.018	0.39	0.142	0.94	0.577
Top marginal tax rate	0.30	0.048	0.03	0.002	**1.00**	**0.410**	0.04	0.002
Controls of the movement of capital and people	0.48	0.037	0.02	0.000	0.13	0.008	0.46	0.044
Standard deviation of inflation	0.80	-0.093	0.92	-0.186	0.05	0.001	0.14	-0.010

(continued)

Table 15. Continued

	LRI		*LTI*		*MTI*		*HTI*	
	PIP	*Post. mean*	*PIP*	*Post. mean*	*PIP*	*Post. mean*	*PIP*	*Post. mean*
Transfers and subsidies	0.14	0.016	0.13	0.017	0.09	0.009	0.06	-0.005
Integrity of the legal system	0.50	0.060	0.12	-0.016	0.13	0.012	0.04	0.000
Impartial courts	0.19	-0.038	0.14	0.042	0.82	-0.322	0.03	0.000
Protection of property rights	0.06	-0.003	**0.97**	**-0.351**	0.12	-0.015	**0.97**	**-0.332**
Government enterprises and investment	0.05	-0.002	0.05	-0.009	0.26	0.069	0.2	-0.049
Regulatory trade barriers	0.04	0.000	0.08	-0.007	0.38	0.040	0.04	0.000

Notes: PIP and Post. mean denote posterior inclusion probability and posterior mean, respectively. The results for regressors with a strong impact on exports (PIP between 0.95 and 1.00) were bolded for convenience.
LRI – Labour-intensive and resource-intensive manufactures
LTI – Low-skill and technology-intensive manufactures
MTI – Medium-skill and technology-intensive manufactures
HTI – High-skill and technology-intensive manufactures
Source: own elaboration.

As regards the result for institutional factors, on the one hand, the more detailed analysis confirms the general conclusion that some institutions play an important role in driving manufacturing exports' competitiveness on international markets, both directly stimulating exports as well as transforming export structures. On the other hand, more detailed analysis of which particular areas of institutions are key to understanding the export performance proves to be more difficult. The strong direct positive impact of Regulation on the export performance seems to stem from a combination of the positive impact of different types of regulations on different types of exports. Business and Labour market regulations seem to be most important for the two extreme categories as regards the skill and technological intensity, but probably for different reasons. As lower regulations increase competition, they have two types of effects: on the one hand, they lower costs of production, allowing less technologically advanced industries to stay in business; on the other hand, they can also stimulate a transition into more innovative industries by encouraging risk-taking or increasing the mobility in the labour market (see e.g. Ranjan et al., 2018; Henrekson, 2020). Credit market regulations are important for the medium skill and technology-intensive exports, which can be related to the need of financing necessary for further development of products in such branches (and potentially reaching a higher level of technological intensity – see e.g. Andersen, 2016).

Low and stable inflation appears to be the most important sub-index of sound monetary conditions for boosting the export performance of the EU countries. As regards freedom to trade internationally, both regulatory trade barriers and tariffs have a significant impact on the overall export performance. They also have some transformational effect on exports as their importance varies with the skill and technology-intensity of exports. The reduction of regulatory trade barriers and tariffs is more beneficial for the exports of more technologically advanced goods. As regards the sub-indices of legal system and property rights, most of them (Impartial courts, Protection of property rights, Integrity of the legal system) do not have an important impact on the export performance, while the impact of higher Judicial independence appears to be negative. The latter seems implausible, and it indicates that in this case one should conclude that in general legal system and property rights has a limited effect on export performance (as in the baseline scenario). Finally, as in the case of the overall measure of the Size of the Government, its sub-indices (Government consumption, Transfers and subsidies, Government enterprises and investment, Top marginal tax rate) do not seem to strongly affect exports.

4.5.3 Does membership in the European Union affect the export performance?

In order to establish whether EU accession has improved export performance, I have added the NMS binary variable that takes the value of 1 for the countries that joined the EU in 2004 or later starting from the year when they entered the EU and is 0 otherwise. I have chosen to use the NMS dummy, rather than the EU membership binary variable, as the latter would be perfectly correlated with country Fixed Effects for all "old" EU member states (see also Schnatz et al. (2005)). The NMS dummy has a PIP over 95 % threshold indicating that joining the EU has had additional benefits for exporters in the NMS; however, nearly all baseline results remain qualitatively the same, except for the impact of the freedom to trade internationally, which has now become only transformational.

Table 16. Baseline results with New Member States Binary Variable

	Total manufactures		*LRI*		*LTI*		*MTI*		*HTI*	
	PIP	*Post. mean*	*PIP*	*Post. mean*	*PIP*	*Post. mean*	*PIP*	*Post. mean*	*PIP*	*Post. mean*
Price competitiveness										
Std. deviation of NEER	0.07	0.00	0.15	0.00	0.05	0.00	0.26	-0.01	0.09	0.00
ULC	0.07	-0.01	0.11	-0.01	0.86	-0.68	0.05	0.00	0.07	-0.01
Technological factors and human capital										
Patent applications	**1.00**	**0.22**	**1.00**	**0.19**	**1.00**	**0.22**	**1.00**	**0.27**	**1.00**	**0.23**
Potential GDP	**0.96**	**0.16**	0.11	0.00	**0.99**	**0.30**	0.74	0.12	**1.00**	**0.36**
FDI stock	**1.00**	**-0.12**	**1.00**	**-0.22**	**1.00**	**0.13**	**1.00**	**-0.21**	**1.00**	**-0.16**
Capital output ratio	0.87	-0.26	0.39	-0.09	0.05	0.00	0.06	0.00	0.48	-0.16
R&D expenditure	0.07	0.00	**1.00**	**-0.22**	**0.97**	**0.27**	0.07	0.00	0.86	0.18
School life expectancy	0.05	0.00	0.84	-0.48	0.88	0.73	0.06	0.00	0.06	0.01
Population with tertiary education	0.06	0.00	**1.00**	**-0.26**	**0.96**	**-0.34**	0.05	0.00	0.22	0.03
Institutional factors										
Regulation	**1.00**	**0.81**	**1.00**	**1.04**	0.09	0.02	**1.00**	**1.06**	**0.99**	**0.00**
Sound money	**0.98**	**0.17**	**1.00**	**0.35**	0.05	0.00	**1.00**	**0.36**	0.08	-0.01
Freedom to Trade Internationally	0.50	0.27	**1.00**	**-1.24**	0.05	-0.01	**0.98**	**0.98**	**1.00**	**1.49**
Legal system and property rights	0.45	-0.19	0.13	-0.02	0.43	-0.32	0.10	-0.02	0.83	-0.67
Size of government	0.12	0.01	**0.99**	**0.29**	0.18	-0.04	0.97	0.28	0.07	0.01
Other factors										
New Member State of the EU	**1.00**	**0.26**	0.83	0.08	0.07	0.01	**1.00**	**0.40**	**1.00**	**0.41**

Notes: PIP and Post. mean denote posterior inclusion probability and posterior mean, respectively. The results for regressors with a strong impact on exports (PIP between 0.95 and 1.00) were bolded for convenience. The NMS binary variable takes the value of 1 for the countries that joined the EU in 2004 or later, starting from the year when they entered the EU, and is 0 otherwise.
LRI – Labour-intensive and resource-intensive manufactures
LTI – Low-skill and technology-intensive manufactures
MTI – Medium-skill and technology-intensive manufactures
HTI – High-skill and technology-intensive manufactures

I have also studied the effect of potential non-linearities and interactions terms (see Table 26 in the Appendix), however my results indicate that there is a rather limited evidence of (selective) non-linear effects of institutions on export performance. Interactions appear to have some meaning in the case of the more skill-intensive and technology-intensive manufactures, where institutions can indirectly affect the export performance by modifying the impact of non-price factors such as the R&D intensity and the FDI stock. These results are stable with respect to the prior assumptions within the BMA framework.

Last but not least, one might expect countries with higher export market shares to have higher potential GDP, since export market share might be highly correlated with the productivity of the country, which can be a source of endogeneity. As a result, I have also carried out the robustness analysis for our baseline results (see Table 27), where I have used the lagged potential GDP as an instrument for the current potential GDP. The baseline results hold, although the estimated effect for potential GDP is higher. One can therefore conclude that there is no reverse causality (endogeneity) from exports to potential GDP.

4.6 Conclusions

The economic literature analysing export performance focuses mostly on price competitiveness and, since the seminal finding of Kaldor (1978), on technological factors. The results from this chapter confirm that it is indeed incorrect to look at international competitiveness only in terms of price factors, as one can observe that technological factors have a much greater impact on the export market share. Furthermore, the obtained results provide some insight into the discussion in the earlier literature as to whether patent applications or R&D intensity should be more important as a driver of exports. At the first glance on the overall value of manufactures, it seems that that R&D is more likely to be only indirectly beneficial for export performance, i.e. when it is successful, resulting in a higher number of patent applications. However, a more detailed analysis of different types of manufactures' exports allows me to add an important new finding to the literature on the technological drivers of exports. I show that R&D expenditure can have a significant transformational impact on the export structure, even though it does not have a significant positive impact on overall exports. My results indicate that higher R&D intensity tends to decrease the share of less technology intensive exports, while giving a stronger boost to more skill- and technology-intensive exports. What is more, the results provide some evidence regarding the significance of the size of the production capacity, measured by potential GDP, for exports of the EU countries.

Moreover, I also show that institutions should be analysed as important factors determining export performance. Similarly to the technological factors, institutions can have both a direct positive effect on overall exports as well as a transformational impact (from less to more technologically advanced exports). I show that overall manufactures' exports benefit most from higher level of freedom to trade internationally, improved quality of regulation (credit market, business and labour market) and institutions safeguarding the stability of the value of money (especially those keeping inflation low and stable). The positive impact of freedom to trade internationally on exports is actually the highest among all the factors included in my analysis. At the same time, freedom to trade internationally has also a significant transformational impact on the structure of the exports of the EU countries.

I also show that human capital has a transformational, rather than direct, impact on exports. Finally, I found little evidence for non-linearities or interactions regarding the influence of institutions on export performance.

5 Exchange rate determinants

Even though economic literature has long been discussing the relation between macroeconomic fundamentals and exchange rates, there is no consensus on which theories (models) and variables are the crucial determinants of the exchange rate movements. In this chapter, I will focus on the identification of the key determinants of the real effective exchange rate (REER), with particular attention paid to the theories focusing on the equilibrium exchange rates.

5.1 The economic theory

Economic literature contains various theories regarding the key determinants of the exchange rate movements that indicate the existence of different types of mechanisms describing the relationship between the macroeconomic fundamentals and changes in the exchange rate. First, there is a variety of behavioural equilibrium exchange rate (BEER) models, which aim to establish a behavioural link between the real rate and relevant economic variables (see e.g. MacDonald 1998). For example, the BEER relation between the exchange rate (denoted as ner_t) can be given by the equation:

$$ner_t = \alpha_0 + \beta_1 gdp_t + \beta_2 tot_t + \beta_3 nfa_t + \beta_4 \widetilde{gdebt}_t + \beta_5 \tilde{p}_t \qquad (32)$$

where gdp_t is the GDP per capita, tot_t denotes terms of trade, nfa_t is the net foreign assets, the $\widetilde{gdebt}_t$ is the relative (intercountry difference) general government debt and $\tilde{p}_t$ denotes relative prices. Such a model can also be further extended to incorporate additional variables.

It is also worth mentioning about the Macroeconomic balances (MB) approach developed by Faruqee et al. (1999) and further extended by the IMF in the External Balance Assessment (EBA) framework in Cubeddu et al. (2019), which focuses on the macroeconomic balance of the economy. The equilibrium exchange rate in the EBA approach can be treated as the value of the exchange rate that allows for a stabilisation of the current account at the target level. As a result, the deviation of the exchange rate from the equilibrium in the EBA framework can be used to predict the future movements of the current account:

$$rer_t = rer_t^{eq} + \frac{ca_t - ca_t^{norm}}{\eta_t} \tag{33}$$

Where rer_t^{eq} denotes equilibrium real exchange rate, ca_t denotes the current account balance and the ca_t^{norm} is the targeted level of the current account balance. The η_t measures the speed of the adjustment mechanism.

Exchange rates can also be studied on the basis of the relative purchasing power parity (PPP), which indicates that the exchange rate reacts to the changes in the intercountry price levels differences:

$$ner_t = \alpha_0 + p_t - p_t^* \tag{34}$$

$$rer_t = rer_t^{PPP} \tag{35}$$

where the p_t the analysed country price level and the p_t^* denotes the price level in the partner country. Ca' Zorzi et al. (2016); Ca' Zorzi et al. (2020) showed that the long-term mean can be used to approximate the PPP equilibrium rate rer_t^{PPP} and the PPP deviations can successfully be used to forecast exchange rates.

Another potential extension of the exchange rate model can be based on the Taylor (1993) rule fundamentals:

$$rer_{t+1} - rer_t = \alpha_0 + \beta_1 \tilde{y}_t + \beta_2 \tilde{\pi}_t \tag{36}$$

where the $\tilde{y}_t$ is the relative output gap and the relative inflation rate is given by $\tilde{\pi}_t$. Monetary policy rule proposed by Taylor (1993) can also be used as a substitute for the monetary policy interest rate as in the Molodtsova and Papell (2009).

The exchange rate can also be modelled using the Uncovered interest parity (UIP). According to this theory, the exchange rate should adjust accordingly to the difference in the interest rates between the two countries. This theory alone seems to be insufficient to explain exchange rate movements, however, some studies (see e.g. Chinn and Meredith, 2004) indicate that UIP can be used to for long-term forecasts.

As regards estimation, the relation between exchange rates and fundamentals can be measured using cointegration relation between the macroeconomic framework (Wdowiński, 2011), the VAR model (Grabowski and Welfe, 2019) or the panel data framework (Dąbrowski et al., 2014).

There is also a strain in the literature that focuses on expectations and animal spirits. For instance, Kaltenbrunner (2015); Barbosa et al. (2018) indicate that aggregate expectations, that can be approximated by yield curve or liquidity premium differential, also have a profound impact on the exchange rate movements, especially in the case of developing and emerging countries. Moreover, Chojnowski and Dybka (2017) propose a novel two-step approach to account for economic sentiments. They begin with the estimation of the economic sentiments and then they apply the obtained measure in the VAR framework that offers improved exchange rate forecasting capabilities compared to a random walk.

In general, the literature on the relation between the macroeconomic fundamentals and exchange rates is continually growing, and therefore the summary above provides only a brief discussion on different modelling approaches. Nevertheless, it allows the identification of a list of potential exchange rate determinants.

5.2 Variable description

Below I outline the list of potential real effective exchange rate determinants along with a brief discussion on their theoretical expected signs. The positive sign indicates an appreciation of the exchange rate.

- **GDP per capita (PPP).** Early studies, such as Harrod (1933), followed by (Balassa, 1964; Samuelson, 1964), focused on the importance of the economic development on the exchange rate and the relative prices. Based on the Harrod-Balassa-Samuelson effect, one can expect appreciation of the exchange rates of the developing economies. Expected sign: positive.
- **Real GDP growth.** The sign of this variable depends on the growth source (mechanism at work). On the one hand, the increase in the GDP growth stemming from export stimulus can be associated with a counterbalancing appreciation of the rate. On the other hand, the increase in GDP that leads to an increase in import can lead to a depreciation of the exchange rate. Expected sign: ambiguous.

- **Net foreign assets to GDP ratio.** Increase in the net foreign assets value leads to higher interest income on the current account that is often counterbalanced by the deterioration of the trade balance. A change in the trade balance, in turn, requires an appreciation of the exchange rate. Expected sign: positive.
- **Current account balance.** Current account adjustment mechanism discussed in the Macroeconomic Balance approach implies that the increase in the current account balance should be accompanied by exchange rate appreciation. Expected sign: positive.
- **Inflation CPI.** A delay in the adjustment mechanism of the nominal exchange rate means that increase in the inflation rate will be accompanied by a depreciation of the real exchange rate. Expected sign: negative.
- **Composite leading indicator** (CLI). This measure should indicate the expected changes in the macroeconomic environment. In general, improvement of the market sentiments should result in higher demand for the currency of the country. Expected sign: positive.
- **General government gross debt to GDP ratio.** The higher level of debt affects the market perception of fiscal risk of a country and can lead to exchange rate depreciation. Expected sign: negative.
- **General government budget balance to GDP ratio.** Increase in budget balance should lower the perceived fiscal risk of a country and lead to exchange rate appreciation. Expected sign: negative.
- **Unemployment rate.** The unemployment rate can be viewed as a measure of the business cycle position. Expected sign: ambiguous.
- **Terms of trade.** A rise in terms of trade should improve the trade balance and therefore lead to exchange rate strengthening. Expected sign: positive.
- **FDI inflows.** Increase in foreign investment value increases the demand for currency, leading to its exchange rate appreciation. Expected sign: positive.

5.3 The data

For the purposes of the analysis, I have created database covering the Eurozone and 21 countries[10] over years 2000–2019 (annual frequency), using the following sources (see Table 17):

Table 17. Definitions of variables used in the analysis

Variable	*Description*	*Source*
REER	Real Effective Exchange Rate, Index 2010=100, logarithm	BIS
GDP per capita	GDP per capita expressed in constant international dollars (purchasing power parity), logarithm	IMF WEO
GDP growth rate	Real gross domestic product annual growth rate	IMF WEO
NFA	Net foreign assets, % of GDP	Own-calculations based on Lane and Milesi-Ferretti (2007)
Current account	Current account balance, % of GDP	IMF WEO
Inflation CPI	Consumer Price Index Inflation rate, % year over year	IMF WEO/IFS
CLI	Composite leading indicator developed by OECD, Index (logarithm)	OECD
Government debt	General government gross debt, % of the GDP	IMF WEO
Government budget	General government budget balance, % of the GDP	IMF WEO
Unemployment	Unemployment rate, %	IMF WEO, ILO
Terms of trade	Terms of trade, index (logarithm)	IMF WEO/IFS, World Bank
FDI inflow	FDI inward flows, % of GDP	OECD

Source: own elaboration.

10 Australia, Brazil, Canada, Chile, China, the Czech Republic, Hungary, Iceland, India, Indonesia, Israel, Japan, Korea, Mexico, Norway, Poland, Russia, South Africa, Switzerland, Turkey, United Kingdom and the United States.

Table 18 provides a brief summary of the data used in the analysis. One can observe that, on average, analysed countries showed substantial volatility of the REER as the average standard deviation among the analysed countries was equal to 10.2 %. Large differences in the GDP per capita and GDP growth rates show that the analysed sample covers both developing (e.g. India, Indonesia) and developed countries. Substantial budget deficits visible in the data are the result of the 2008–2009 Recession. A similar explanation can also be provided for the high level of the maximum unemployment rate. The highest level of CPI Inflation was observed in Turkey at the beginning of the sample (years 2000–2001). The enormous negative net foreign assets position and current account deficits were observed in Iceland before 2009.

Table 18. Statistical summary of the data used in this chapter

	Min	*Max*	*Mean*	*Std. deviation*
REER	53.7	153.9	96.3	10.2
GDP growth rate	-7.8	14.3	3.3	2.2
GDP per capita	2546	66948	28819	2883
Current account	-23.1	16.3	0.2	2.5
Inflation CPI	-1.4	55.0	4.0	2.5
CLI	93.3	106.2	100.0	1.3
Government debt	3.9	237.7	56.4	12.3
Government budget	-13.2	18.7	-1.9	2.4
Unemployment	1.7	27.9	7.2	1.5
Terms of trade	62.3	144.8	101.1	8.2
FDI inflow	-11.7	31.7	2.8	2.0
NFA	-661.0	205.1	-17.8	23.8

Source: own elaboration.

5.4 Baseline results

My baseline specification of the REER model is estimated with a *Zellner's g-prior* based on "Unit Information Prior" criterion (see chapter 2 for technical details). In the case of the prior model size, I assume binomial-beta prior that results in uniform prior probability for model size. The mean posterior model size is approximately 4.5 (see Figure 10).

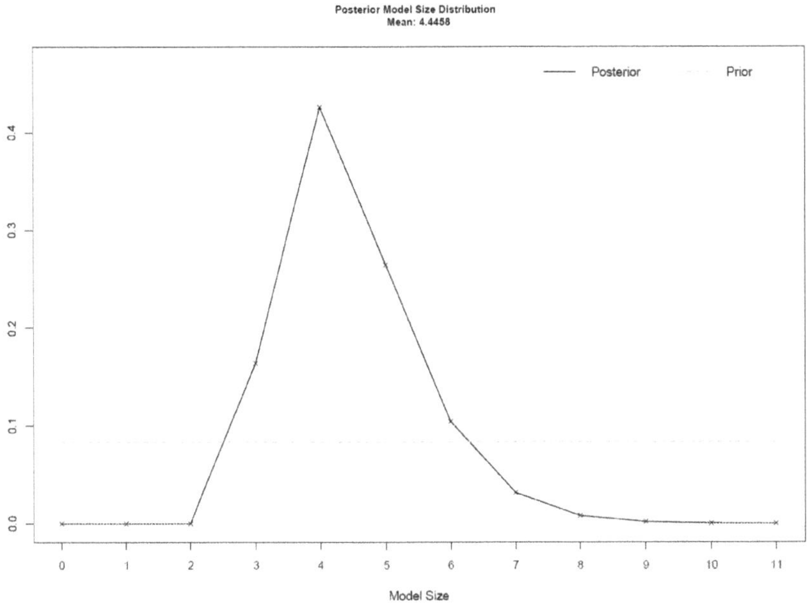

Figure 10. Posterior model size
Source: own elaboration.

The graphical visualisation of the obtained results presented in Figure 11 shows that three variables have posterior inclusion probability very close to 1, namely terms of trade, general government debt and the GDP per capita. The following variable, consumer price inflation, also has a substantial PIP although some white spots are visible. The remaining variables seem to have a much lesser impact on the real exchange rate. Such a result can be viewed as evidence supporting the BEER approach to REER modelling. Moreover, the coefficient signs of the top four variables are also in line with expectations outlined in chapter 5.2.

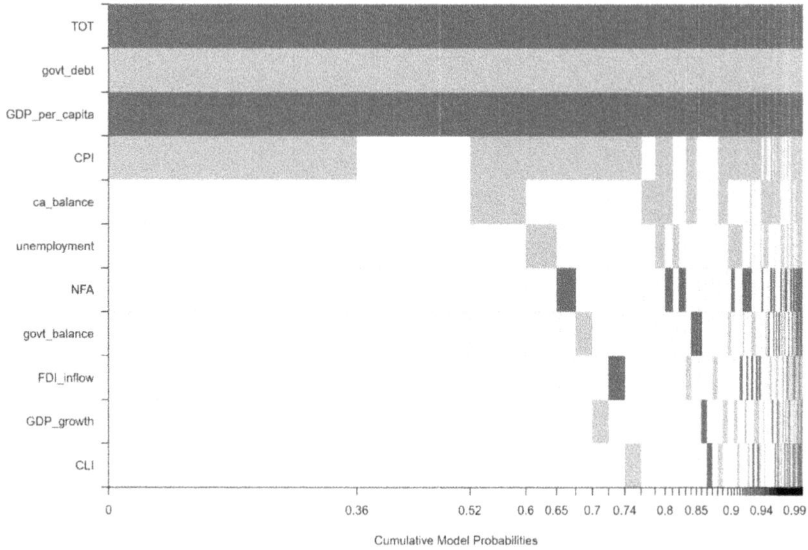

Figure 11. Variable selection
Notes: Light gray colour indicates negative sign (depreciation) and dark gray colour indicates positive sign.
Source: own elaboration.

To get a more detailed view of the BMA analysis results, I have also presented posterior inclusion probabilities and the weighted mean values of the coefficients obtained for the REER determinants in Table 19. In the model specification, I have used the logarithms of the REER, terms of trade and the composite Leading indicator. On the one hand, obtained results indicate that improvement in terms of trade by 1 % leads to an exchange rate appreciation equal to 0.37 % (assuming that other factors are kept constant). Moreover, the increase in GDP per capita equal to 1000USD (adjusted for purchasing power parity) can be associated with 0.17 % appreciation of the currency. On the other hand, the increase in Government debt by 1 % of GDP leads to an exchange rate deterioration by 0.285 %. It is also worth looking at the Inflation CPI, where the coefficient equal to -0.25 indicates that the adjustment of the nominal rate to the change of inflation is not immediate, leading to a minor deprecation of the REER.

Table 19. REER determinants: baseline approach

	PIP	*Post. Mean*
Terms of trade	**1.0000**	**0.3700**
Government debt	**1.0000**	**-0.2854**
GDP per capita	**1.0000**	**0.1661**
Inflation CPI	0.7434	-0.2479
Current account	0.2001	-0.0478
Unemployment	0.1207	-0.0347
NFA	0.0877	0.0005
Government budget	0.0754	-0.0007
FDI inflow	0.0737	-0.0009
GDP growth rate	0.0728	-0.0016
CLI	0.0720	-0.0002

Notes: PIP and Post. mean denote posterior inclusion probability and posterior mean, respectively. The results for regressors with a strong impact on REER (PIP between 0.95 and 1.00) were bolded for convenience.

Source: own elaboration.

5.5 Sensitivity analysis regarding prior assumptions

In the sensitivity analysis I check how stable are the baseline results with respect to the choice of models prior using the two scenarios as in chapters 3.5.1 and 4.5.3. The main conclusion of this exercise is that the choice of prior has minimal effect on the estimates. I can observe only minor changes in the values of the PIP, which indicates that my results are robust concerning different choices of prior assumptions on the model size and inclusion probability of the variables. In the unconservative scenario, the PIPs are generally higher, but there is no new variable that exceeds the 95 % threshold.

Table 20. Sensitivity of the results with respect to the prior assumptions

	Baseline assumptions		*Conservative assumptions*		*Unconservative assumptions*	
	PIP	*Post. mean*	*PIP*	*Post. mean*	*PIP*	*Post. mean*
Terms of trade	**1.00**	**0.3700**	**1.00**	**0.3716**	**1.00**	**0.3686**
Government debt	**1.00**	**-0.2854**	**1.00**	**-0.2888**	**1.00**	**-0.2802**
GDP per capita	**1.00**	**0.1661**	**1.00**	**0.1695**	**1.00**	**0.1602**
Inflation CPI	0.74	-0.2479	0.63	-0.2081	0.93	-0.3159
Current account	0.20	-0.0478	0.10	-0.0232	0.44	-0.1096
Unemployment	0.12	-0.0347	0.06	-0.0149	0.29	-0.0874
NFA	0.09	0.0005	0.04	0.0002	0.22	0.0013
Government budget	0.08	-0.0007	0.03	-0.0001	0.19	-0.0017
FDI inflow	0.07	-0.0009	0.03	0.0000	0.18	-0.0045
GDP growth rate	0.07	-0.0016	0.03	-0.0002	0.18	-0.0062
CLI	0.07	-0.0002	0.03	0.0004	0.18	-0.0023

Notes: PIP and Post. mean denote posterior inclusion probability and posterior mean, respectively. The results for regressors with a strong impact on REER (PIP between 0.95 and 1.00) were bolded for convenience.

Source: own elaboration.

Obtained results confirm that variables often used in the behavioural equilibrium exchange rate framework are indeed essential determinants of the real exchange rate movements. The highest levels of the posterior inclusion probabilities were observed for terms of trade, general government debt and the GDP per capita. In addition to this, consumer price inflation also has a substantial PIP indicating that nominal exchange rates reaction to an increase in inflation is immediate and higher inflation can lead to depreciation of the real effective exchange rate.

5.6 Can exchange rate determinants differ in time?

The complexity of the relation between the macroeconomic variables leads to a situation that economic models based on macroeconomic fundamentals often fail to outperform the forecasting capabilities of the random walk (see, e.g. Meese and Rogoff, 1983), which is called *exchange rate disconnect puzzle*. This leads to a question of potential sources of such outcome. One potential explanation is that exchange rate depend on various macroeconomic variables and their importance can change in time Dybka (2020).

As a result, I would like to conduct additional test of the stability of obtained results. In this part, I will focus on five major currencies, namely CAD, EUR, CHF, GBP and JPY and their nominal exchange rate against the US dollar. Since these are highly developed economies, there is more data available, so I extend the dataset to cover the 1980–2018 period at a quarterly frequency (see Table 21).

Table 21. Potential determinants of the exchange rate movements and their data sources

Variable	*Source*
Exchange rate	IMF IFS
GDP growth rate	IMF WEO; interpolated
GDP per capita (PPP)	IMF WEO; interpolated
Output gap	OECD, IMF; interpolated
Current account balance	IMF (IFS; WEO; interpolation)
M2 money supply	FRED, central bank databases
Inflation CPI	IMF IFS
Composite leading indicator	OECD
General government debt	IMF WEO; interpolated
General government deficit	IMF WEO; interpolated
Output per worker	IMF and ILO data
Unemployment rate	ILO
PPP exchange rate	IMF WEO; interpolated
Terms of trade	IMF IFS
FDI inflow (% of GDP)	IMF WEO; interpolated
Net foreign assets (% of GDP)	Lane and Milesi-Ferretti (2007); interpolated
Monetary policy rate (3 month rate)	Wu-Xia and RBNZ shadow rates; FRED, central bank databases
10 year gov't bond yield	FRED, central bank databases

Source: own elaboration.

Such an extended, quarterly dataset allows me to use the Dynamic Bayesian model averaging (see section 2.5) and study the stability of posterior inclusion probabilities.

Determinants of the USD/CAD rate

In the case of the USD/CAD rate, the lagged exchange rate retains high PIP over the sample, indicating that there is significant persistency in the exchange rate. Furthermore, output per worker, terms of trade and purchasing power parity remain highly important over the whole sample. In contrast, government deficit, net foreign assets (NFA), GDP growth and GDP per capita[11] have increased their posterior inclusion probabilities after the year 2000. The remaining variables had lower PIP values and can be found in Figure 22 in the Appendix.

11 Interestingly, the GDP per capita has much lower PIP value as in the static, panel approach used earlier, where it seemed more important that output per worker.

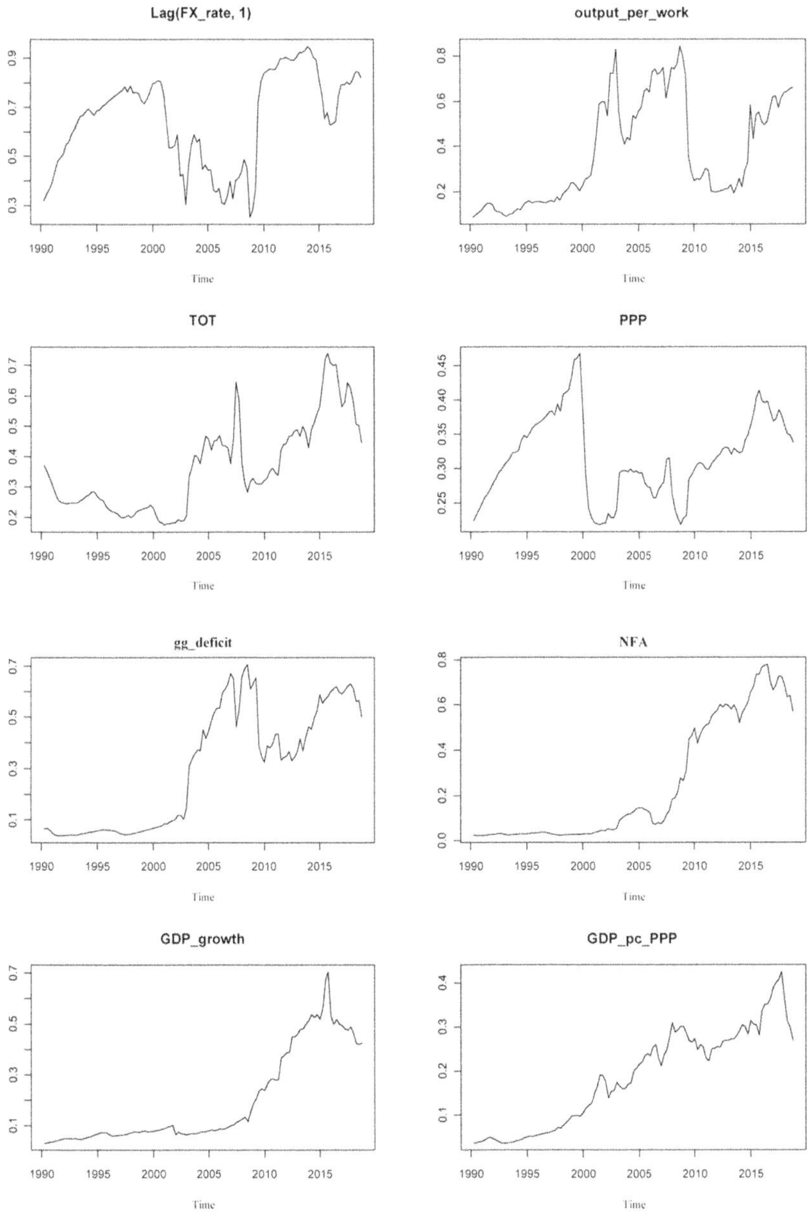

Figure 12. Posterior inclusion probabilities of the key variables for USD/CAD exchange rate forecasts
Source: own elaboration.

The obtained values of posterior inclusion probabilities showed significant volatility over the sample, especially over the last 15 years. This result stems from the fact that the posterior weighted value of forgetting factor, δ, has also decreased over the last year, indicating that more flexibility in the parameter's value was allowed. Such a result can be interpreted as evidence that volatility in the CAD/USD market has increased over the last years. What is more, there is a visible drop in the δ value in the periods of the last economic crisis (Great Recession) indicating that some structural changes took place after the crisis.

Figure 13. Posterior weighted average estimate of δ (forgetting factor)
Source: own elaboration.

Determinants of the USD/CHF rate

On the one hand, the results obtained in the case of USD/CHF to some extent resemble the Canadian case. First of all, one can observe that the lagged value of exchange rate, output per worker and purchasing power parity remain highly important over the whole sample. Second, similar to the Canadian dollar, GDP per capita and net foreign assets also gain importance over time, although in the case of Swiss franc the growth in the posterior inclusion probability is more gradual.

On the other hand, there were some essential differences among those countries. Although the PIP of terms of trade was rather high throughout most of the sample, it seems that it had disappeared in the last three years. Moreover, neither government deficit nor the GDP growth proved to be important in the case of the Swiss franc (see Table?? in the Appendix). In the case of the Swiss franc, the ten-year government bond yield and the inflation rate showed high levels of the posterior inclusion probability over the last 15 years.

In order to better understand the changes in the Swiss franc market, I have presented the values of the forgetting factor, δ, measuring the coefficients volatility. One can divide the sample into two periods. Until 2008, the value of δ was increasing, which means that the coefficient values were stabilising. However, after the Great Recession, a decrease in the δ value can be observed, meaning that the Swiss franc market is less stable after the Great Recession.

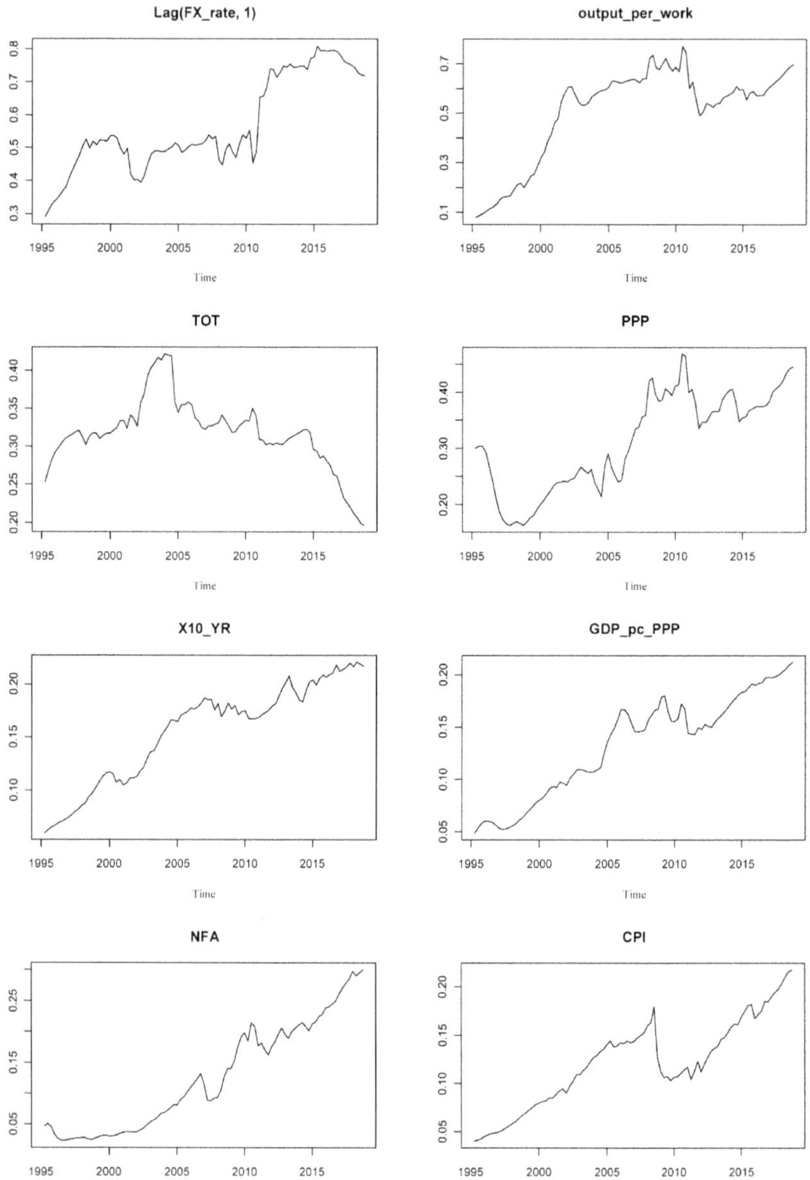

Figure 14. Posterior inclusion probabilities of the key variables for USD/CHF exchange rate forecasts
Source: own elaboration.

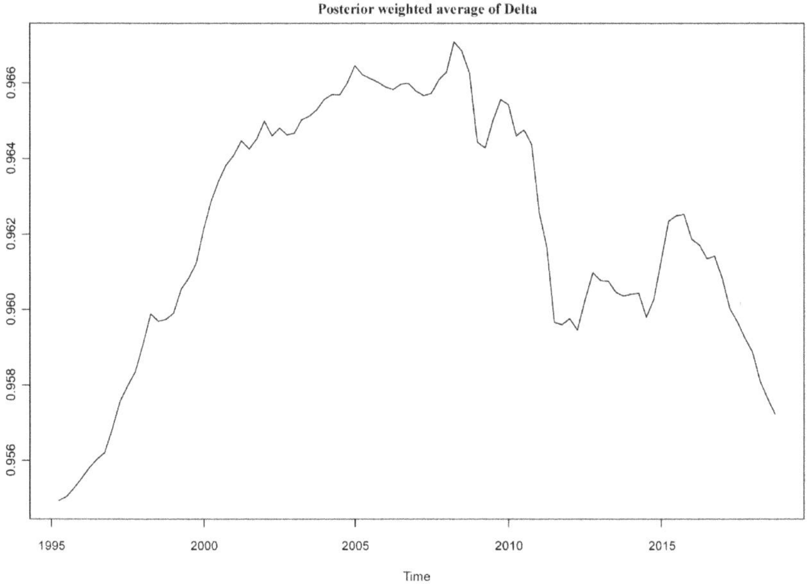

Figure 15. Posterior weighted average estimate of δ (forgetting factor)
Source: own elaboration.

Determinants of the EUR/USD rate

In general, the posterior inclusion probabilities obtained in the case of the EUR/USD are similar to CAD and CHF. The lagged exchange rate, output per worker, terms of trade and purchasing power parity remain highly important over the whole sample. After the Great Recession and the European sovereign debt crisis, one can observe that the general government deficit, current account balance, CPI inflation rate as well as the GDP per capita, have substantially increased their PIP.

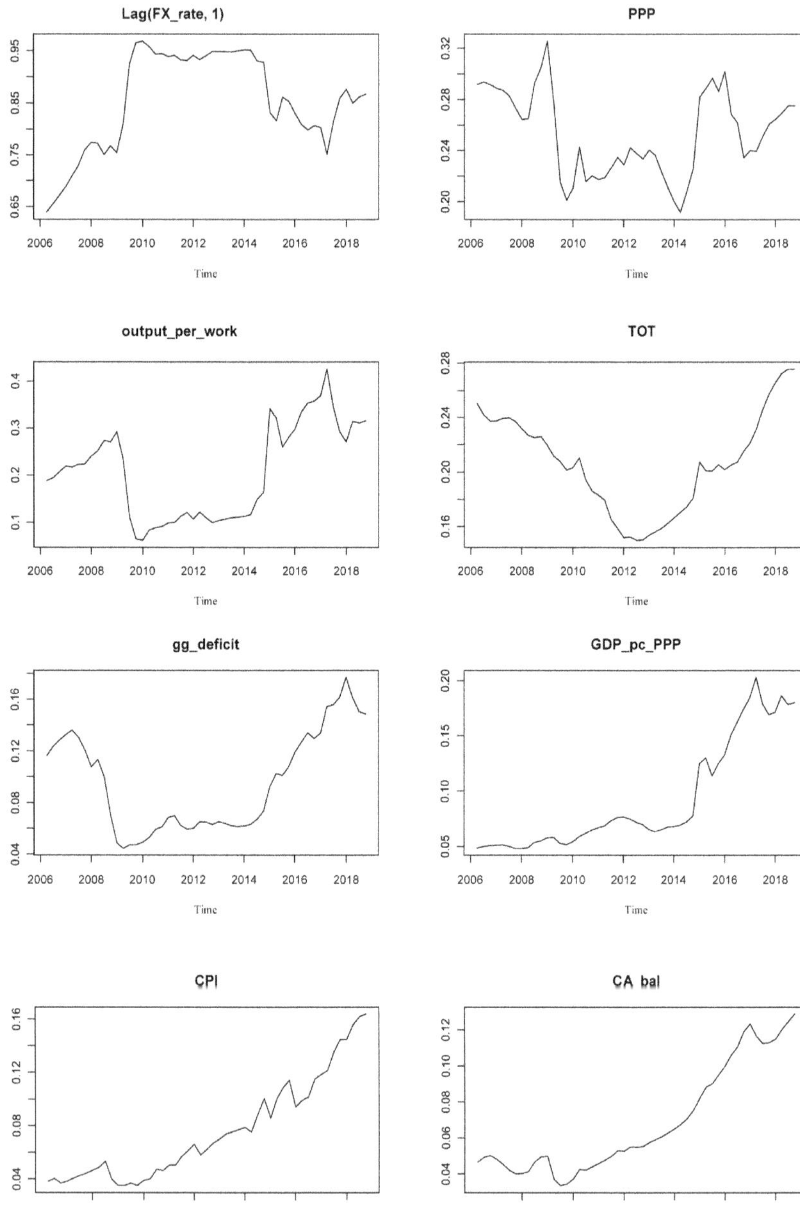

Figure 16. Posterior inclusion probabilities of the key variables for EUR/USD exchange rate forecasts
Source: own elaboration.

The volatility of the Euro has increased after the Great Recession period, which might be the effect of the sovereign debt problems of several euro area members. It is worth noting that at the end of the sample, the value of δ factor has reached higher levels than before the crisis, indicating stabilisation of the EUR/USD market.

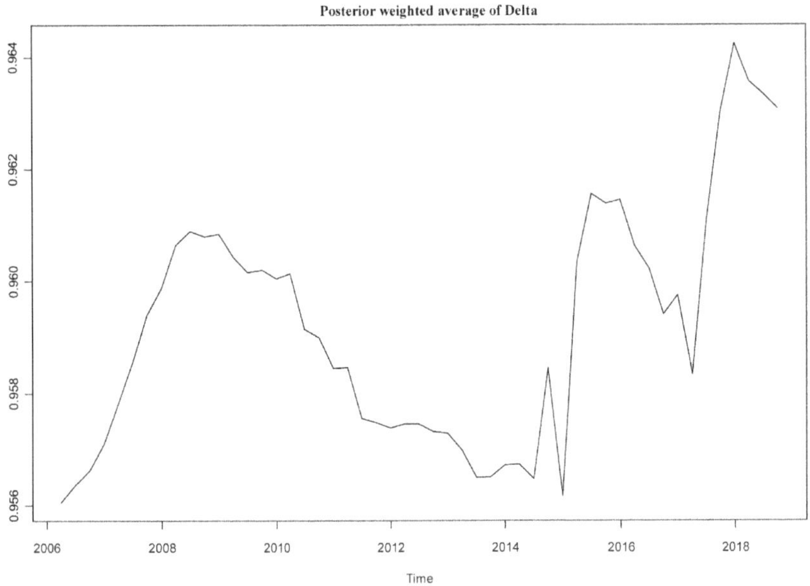

Figure 17. Posterior weighted average estimate of δ (forgetting factor)
Source: own elaboration.

Determinants of the USD/JPY rate

The lagged exchange rate, output per worker, terms of trade and purchasing power parity remain crucial over the whole sample in the case of Japanese Yen. Interestingly, lagged value of economic sentiments, measured with the composite leading indicator (CLI), increased their importance in recent years.

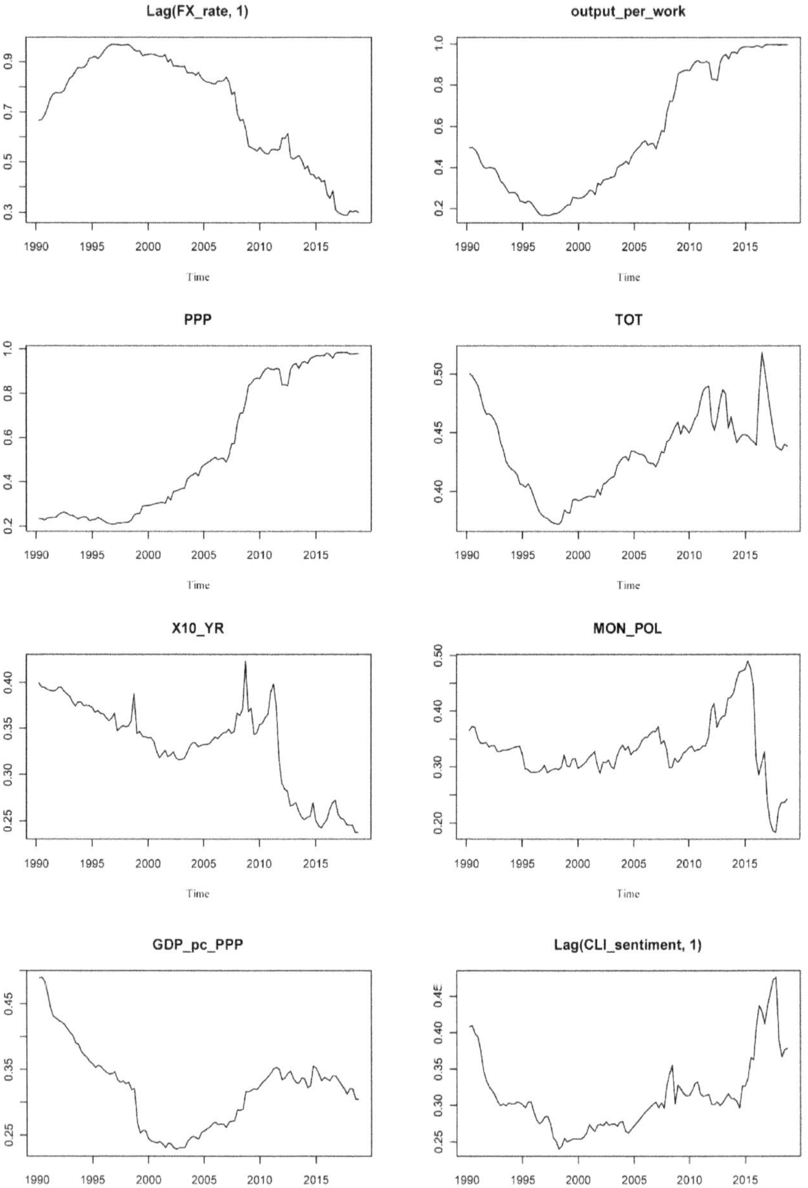

Figure 18. Posterior inclusion probabilities of the key variables for USD/JPY exchange rate forecasts
Source: own elaboration.

In the case of the USD/JPY rate, there is significant volatility of the posterior inclusion probabilities. Since the early 2000s, one can observe a steady decrease of the δ factor, that indicates that volatility of the Japanese yen determinants is increasing.

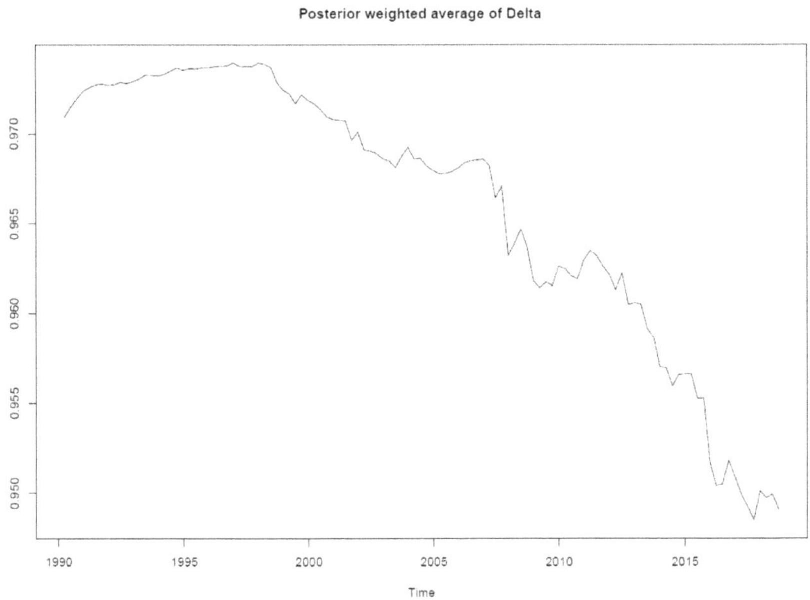

Figure 19. Posterior weighted average estimate of δ (forgetting factor)
Source: own elaboration.

Determinants of the USD/GBP rate

The USD/GDP exchange rate seems to differ the most in comparison with the other analysed currencies. First of all, the lagged exchange rate does not have the highest posterior inclusion probability, indicating that the persistence of the USD/GBP rate seems less profound than in the case of the remaining analysed variables.

Second, the lagged composite leading indicator is among the top variables with respect to the PIP. Only in Japan, this variable was included in the top 8 variables, although its importance differed in time.

Third, the posterior inclusion probability of PPP rate is the lowest among the group of analysed countries. One can observe that in the beginning of the 1990's, the posterior inclusion probability of the PPP rate was close to zero, indicating that only in the more recent data the PPP played a more profound role in shaping the GBP exchange rate.

Fourth, one can also observe substantial structural changes in the aftermath of the recent economic crisis – M2 monetary aggregate, general government debt and deficit saw a considerable increase in their posterior inclusion probability after 2008. Such a result indicates that in the recent year monetary policy theories and behavioural equilibrium exchange rates became more relevant in the case of the British pound.

Although changes in the δ forgetting factor were not substantial through most of the sample, there were two periods when the δ value dropped significantly. The first such period was the Great Recession in 2008–2009 and the second one was prior to the Brexit referendum in 2015, indicating that in those periods some structural changes took place in the British pound market.

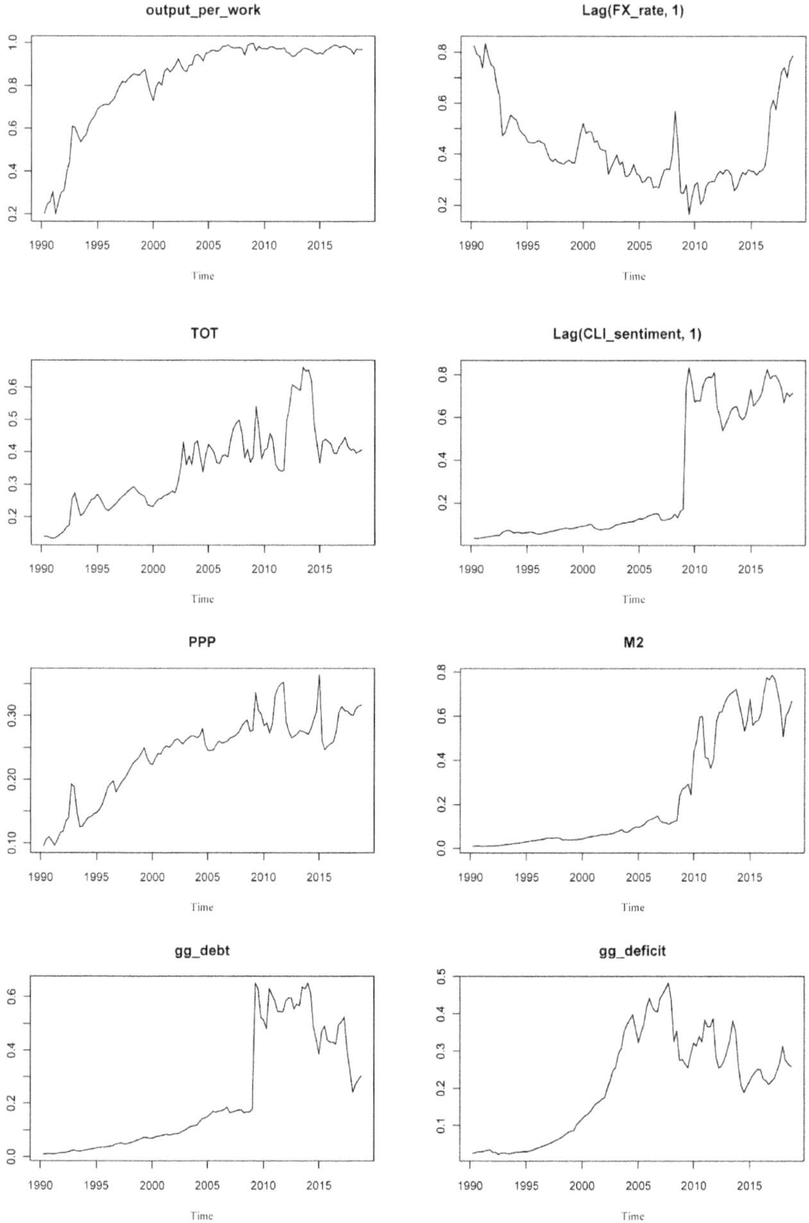

Figure 20. Posterior inclusion probabilities of the key variables for USD/GBP exchange rate forecasts
Source: own elaboration.

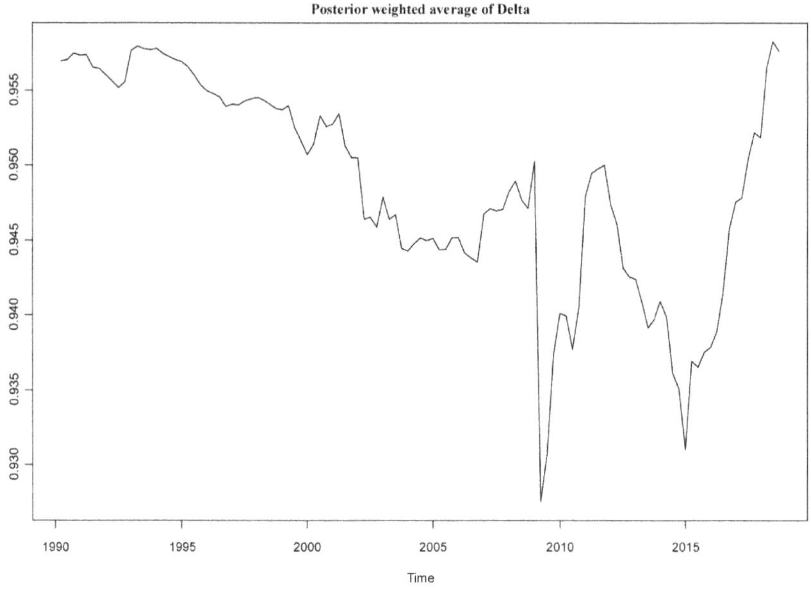

Figure 21. Posterior weighted average estimate of δ (forgetting factor)
Source: own elaboration.

5.7 Conclusions

Obtained results confirm that variables often used in the behavioural equilibrium exchange rate framework are indeed essential determinants of the real exchange rate movements. The highest levels of the posterior inclusion probabilities were observed for terms of trade, general government debt and the GDP per capita. In addition to this, consumer price inflation also has a substantial PIP indicating that nominal exchange rates reaction to an increase in inflation is immediate and higher inflation can lead to depreciation of the real effective exchange rate. Nevertheless, more detailed conclusions require country-specific approach as the set of essential macroeconomic fundamentals can substantially differ both in time and across the countries.

6 Final conclusions

Although some authors, such as Krugman (1994), claim that focusing on the competitiveness of countries is not advisable as it might lead to wrong policies, the same can also be said about focusing on other economic measures, Boltho (1996). In my study, the goal is to better understand the sources of the economy's external stability that could also help sustain economic growth. From this perspective, my focus is not just on maintaining the trade balance or finding the arguments for devaluation of the currency but to understand better what factors lie behind the changes in the international relations between the economies. As a result, I have chosen three measures, namely the current account balance, export market share and the real exchange rate, that can be viewed as from general to specific approach. The current account is the most general measure as it includes international trade balance and capital flows, whereas export market shares are part of the trade balance, and the exchange rate can be viewed as the most detailed (i.e. focusing only on the price channel) measure of the international competitiveness of the economy.

Using the BMA methodology allowed me to account for model uncertainty, i.e. the uncertainty related to selecting variables included in the model. The main advantage of the BMA approach is that I estimate all the possible models for the given combinations of the available variables instead of a single model. For each model in the BMA framework, there is a posterior probability measure that this model reflects the true data generating process. On this basis, I can also obtain the posterior inclusion probability of each variable, which is a straightforward measure of variable importance. Overall, the BMA proved itself a very useful tool in analysing the importance of macroeconomic drivers of current account, export market share and exchange rates.

My results showed that intratemporal factors seem to have a lesser effect on the current account (except the fuel balance variable) than the intertemporal factors, which provides some evidence against the ICA model. On the other hand, the intertemporal factors, namely investment rate, budget balance or relative stage of development, can be viewed as the key drivers of the current account among the intertemporal factors group. This leads me to a conclusion that a permanent (stable) adjustment of the current account balance requires changes in the factors related to economic development and therefore it is a time-consuming, gradual process. As a result, short-term policies focusing on exchange rate adjustment do not seem to be effective.

In addition to this, it is worth noting that there are some profound differences between developing and developed countries in terms of the current account drivers. High-income countries are, to a considerable extent, financing investment and government expenditures with external resources. In turn, for developing countries, the quality of institutions was found to play a more prominent role than in the case of developed countries. Once again, this shows that stable adjustment of current account requires long-term policy tools focusing on improvement of institutional quality. Moreover, the analysis of current account dynamics should take into account both systematic fundamentals – mostly intertemporal factors – as well as country-specific developments.

Next, I have studied the determinants of the manufactures export market share, where I have examined three types of potential determinants of export performance, namely price, technological and institutional factors. The observed effects can be divided into two types: direct and transformational effects. The first category includes situations, where improvement of the investigated measure directly stimulates exports. In contrast, the second type of impact leads to structural changes (improvement leads to shifting from less to more technologically advanced exports).

Obtained results show that technological factors have a much more significant impact on the export market share than price factors. While some technological factors only have a significant transformational impact on the export structure, other factors significantly benefit overall export performance. For example, at first glance on the overall value of manufactures, it seems that the R&D intensity is more likely to be only indirectly beneficial for export performance, i.e. when it is successful, resulting in a higher number of patent applications. However, a more detailed analysis of different types of manufactures' exports indicates that R&D expenditure can have a significant transformational impact on the export structure, even though it does not have a significant positive impact on overall exports.

Higher R&D intensity tends to decrease the share of less technology-intensive exports while giving a more substantial boost to more skill- and technology-intensive exports. The results regarding other factors like foreign direct investment or human capital also point to the importance of taking a holistic view on exports (including services) and of accounting for unique characteristics of analysed countries. Furthermore, the production capacity, measured by potential GDP, also seems vital for exports of the EU countries.

Furthermore, my results also indicate that institutions also play an essential role in shaping the international position of the exporters. Freedom to trade internationally has the highest overall positive impact on manufactures' exports, which seems to be related to the significant impact of lower regulatory trade barriers as well as tariffs. It is also associated with the transformation of export structures (specialisation in more skill- and technology-intensive manufactures), which seems to be mainly related to lower Controls of the movement of capital and people. The second most crucial institution as regards export performance is Regulation. The regulatory environment has a direct positive impact on overall exports, which seems to stem from a combination of the positive impact of different types of regulations on different types of exports. Business and labour market regulations are most important for the two extreme categories of exports as regards skill and technological intensity, which can be explained by the fact that lower product market regulations increase competition and facilitate smooth allocation of resources. Therefore, on the one hand, they lower costs of production and allow less technologically advanced industries to stay in business, while, on the other hand, they reduce margins, thereby encouraging risk-taking and innovation and stimulating transition into more innovative industries (similarly to higher freedom to trade internationally). Credit market regulations are particularly important for the medium skill- and technology-intensive exports, which can be related to the need of financing necessary for investment and accumulation of capital and further development and upgrading of products. Finally, my results show that sound money, notably a low and stable inflation, which supports and preserves gains from trade, also appears to have a strong positive direct impact on overall exports. It is also worth noting that European Union accession (which can also be viewed as an improvement in the country's institutions due to adjusting to regulatory requirements of the EU) is another factor stimulating the export performance, especially in the case of medium and high skill- and technology-intensive manufactures.

Although my results indicate that exchange rates have a limited effect on the current account balance and export market share, I have studied them in greater detail. The most important macroeconomic variables for exchange rate movements analysis seem to include terms of trade, general government debt, and the GDP per capita. In addition to this, consumer price inflation also has a substantial PIP indicating that nominal exchange rates reaction to an increase in inflation is immediate and higher inflation can lead to depreciation of the real effective exchange rate. Nevertheless, I have also tested the usefulness of the (dynamic) Bayesian model averaging in the exchange rate analysis. The results show that nominal exchange rate determinants can substantially differ in time and across the countries. Moreover, the recent Great Recession and the European sovereign debt crisis saw a substantial increase in the exchange rates' volatility, which also led to some structural changes in the crucial determinants of the currency movements. In general, my results show that there is no single characteristic set of crucial determinants of the exchange rates that, to some extent, explains the difficulties in forecasting exchange rates using macroeconomic fundamentals.

Overall, my results indicate that the focus of policy-makers on price competitiveness might be exaggerated. First, current account balance as well as export market share were found to be loosely related to the real effective exchange rate developments. Second, the importance of macroeconomic variables for exchange rates movements can substantially differ in time, which means that they react to current changes in the economic environment rather than track economic changes related to, e.g. economic policy. As such, they are not a good measure of international competitiveness. Moreover, the current account balance and export market shares have shown that they depend on long-term factors such as institutional development. As such, I conclude that the international competitiveness of the economy is a concept closely interlinked with economic development and the factors that lead to economic development also positively affect the economy's competitiveness.

References

Acemoglu, D., Johnson, S., and Robinson, J. A. (2005). "Chapter 6: Institutions as a Fundamental Cause of Long-Run Growth." Volume 1 of *Handbook of Economic Growth*, pp. 385–472. Elsevier.

Alessandrini, P., Fratianni, M., Hughes Hallett, A., and Presbitero, A. (2014). "External imbalances and fiscal fragility in the euro area." *Open Economies Review*, 25(1): 3–34.

Alvarez, J. and Arellano, M. (2003). "The time series and cross-section asymptotics of dynamic panel data estimators." *Econometrica*, 71(4): 1121–1159.

Amable, B. and Verspagen, B. (1995). "The role of technology in market shares dynamics." *Applied Economics*, 27(2): 197–204.

Amendola, G., Dosi, G., and Papagni, E. (1993). "The dynamics of international competitiveness." *Review of World Economics (Weltwirtschaftliches Archiv)*, 129(3): 451–471.

Andersen, D. C. (2016). "Credit constraints, technology upgrading, and the environment." *Journal of the Association of Environmental and Resource Economists*, 3(2): 283–319.

Anderton, B. (1999). "Innovation, product quality, variety, and trade performance: an empirical analysis of Germany and the UK." *Oxford Economic Papers*, 51(1): 152– 167.

Balassa, B. (1964). "The purchasing-power parity doctrine: A reappraisal." *Journal of Political Economy*, 72(6): 584–596.

Barbosa, L. O. S., Jr., F. G. J., and Missio, F. J. (2018). "Determinants of the real exchange rate in the long-run for developing and emerging countries: A theoretical and empirical approach." *International Review of Applied Economics*, 32(1): 62–83.

Bierut, B. K. and Dybka, P. (2021). "Increase versus transformation of exports through technological and institutional innovation: Evidence from bayesian model averaging." *Economic Modelling*, 99: 105501.

Bierut, B. K. and Kuziemska-Pawlak, K. (2017). "Competitiveness and Export Performance of CEE Countries." *Eastern European Economics*, 55(6): 522–542.

Blanchard, O. and Giavazzi, F. (2002). "Current account deficits in the euro area: The end of the Feldstein Horioka puzzle?" *Brookings Papers on Economic Activity*, 33(2): 147–210.

Blanchard, O. and Milesi-Ferretti, G. M. (2010). "Global imbalances: In midstream?" *CEPR Discussion Papers 7693*, C.E.P.R. Discussion Papers.

Boltho, A. (1996). "The assessment: international competitiveness." *Oxford Review of Economic Policy*, 12(3): 1–16.

Bournakis, I. (2014). "Costs, knowledge and market structure: Understanding the puzzle of international competitiveness with Greek export data." *International Review of Applied Economics*, 28(2): 240–269.

Bournakis, I. and Tsoukis, C. (2016). "Government size, institutions, and export performance among OECD economies." *Economic Modelling*, 53: 37–47.

Bussière, M., Fratzscher, M., and Müller, G. J. (2010). "Productivity shocks, budget deficits and the current account." *Journal of International Money and Finance*, 29(8): 1562–1579.

Ca' Zorzi, M., Cap, A., Mijakovic, A., and Rubaszek, M. (2020). "The predictive power of equilibrium exchange rate models." *Working Paper Series 2358*, European Central Bank.

Ca' Zorzi, M. and Rubaszek, M. (2012). "On the empirical evidence of the intertemporal current account model for the euro area countries." *Review of Development Economics*, 16(1): 95–106.

Carlin, W., Glyn, A., and Van Reenen, J. (2001). "Export Market Performance of OECD Countries: An Empirical Examination of the Role of Cost Competitiveness." *Economic Journal*, 111(468): 128–162.

Ca' Zorzi, M., Mućk, J., and Rubaszek, M. (2016). "Real Exchange Rate Forecasting and PPP: This Time the Random Walk Loses." *Open Economies Review*, 27(3): 585–609.

Ca'Zorzi, M., Chudik, A., and Dieppe, A. (2012). "Thousands of models, one story: Current account imbalances in the global economy." *Journal of International Money and Finance*, 31(6): 1319–1338.

Chen, R., Milesi-Ferretti, G.-M., and Tressel, T. (2012). "External Imbalances in the Euro Area." *IMF Working Papers 12/236*, International Monetary Fund.

Chinn, M. (2006). "A Primer on Real Effective Exchange Rates: Determinants, Overvaluation, Trade Flows and Competitive Devaluation." *Open Economies Review*, 17(1): 115–143.

Chinn, M. D. and Meredith, G. (2004). "Monetary Policy and Long-Horizon Uncovered Interest Parity." *IMF Staff Papers*, 51(3): 409–430.

Chinn, M. D. and Prasad, E. S. (2003). "Medium-term determinants of current accounts in industrial and developing countries: An empirical exploration." *Journal of International Economics*, 59(1): 47–76.

Chojnowski, M. and Dybka, P. (2017). "Is Exchange Rate Moody? Forecasting Exchange Rate with Google Trends Data." *Econometric Research in Finance*, 2(1): 1–21.

Cieślik, A. and Hagemejer, J. (2011). "The Effectiveness of Preferential Trade Liberalization in Central and Eastern Europe." Working Paper 61, Faculty of Economic Sciences, University of Warsaw.

Cieślik, A. and Parteka, A. (2018). "Export Variety, Productivity, and Country Size in a Multi-Good Ricardian Model of Export Diversification." GUT FME Working Paper Series A 52, Faculty of Management and Economics, Gdansk University of Technology.

Crozet, M., Milet, E., and Mirza, D. (2016). "The impact of domestic regulations on international trade in services: Evidence from firm-level data." *Journal of Comparative Economics*, 44(3): 585–607.

Cubeddu, L. M., Krogstrup, S., Adler, G., Rabanal, P., Dao, M. C., Hannan, S. A., Juvenal, L., Buitron, C. O., Rebillard, C., Garcia-Macia, D., Jones, C., Rodriguez, J., Chang, K. S., Gautam, D., and Wang, Z. (2019). "The External Balance Assessment Methodology: 2018 Update." *IMF Working Papers 2019/065*, International Monetary Fund.

Dornbusch, R. (1996). "The effectiveness of exchange-rate changes." *Oxford Review of Economic Policy*, 12(3): 26–38.

Dosi, G., Grazzi, M., and Moschella, D. (2015). "Technology and costs in international competitiveness: From countries and sectors to firms." *Research Policy*, 44(10): 1795–1814.

Dybka, P. (2020). "One model or many? Exchange rates determinants and their predictive capabilities." *Working Papers 2020–053*, Warsaw School of Economics, Collegium of Economic Analysis.

Dybka, P. and Rubaszek, M. (2017). "What Determines the Current Account: Intratemporal versus Intertemporal Factors." *Czech Journal of Economics and Finance (Finance a uver)*, 67(1): 2–14.

Dąbrowski, M. A., Papież, M., and Śmiech, S. (2014). "Exchange rates and monetary fundamentals in CEE countries: Evidence from a panel approach." *Journal of Macroeconomics*, 41: 148–159.

European Commission (2012). "Current account surpluses in the EU." *European economy No. 9*, European Commission.

Fagerberg, J. (1988). "International competitiveness." *The Economic Journal*, 98(391): 355–374.

Fagerberg, J. (1996). "Technology and Competitiveness." *Oxford Review of Economic Policy*, 12(3): 39–51.

Faruqee, H., Isard, P., and Masson, P. R. (1999). *A Macroeconomic Balance Framework for Estimating Equilibrium Exchange Rates*, pp. 103–133. Springer Netherlands, Dordrecht.

Foster, D. P. and George, E. I. (1994). "The risk inflation criterion for multiple regression." *The Annals of Statistics*, 22(4): 1947–1975.

Fratianni, M. (2009). *The Gravity Equation in International Trade*. Oxford University Press.

Gilbert, J. and Muchová, E. (2018). "Export competitiveness of Central and Eastern Europe since the enlargement of the EU." *International Review of Economics & Finance*, 55(C): 78–85.

Grabowski, W. and Welfe, A. (2019). "The tobit cointegrated vector autoregressive model: An application to the currency market." *Economic Modelling*.

Hagemejer, J. (2018). "Trade and Growth in the New Member States: The Role of Global Value Chains." *Emerging Markets Finance and Trade*, 54(11): 2630–2649.

Harrod, R. (1933). *International Economics*. Nisbet & Cambridge University Press.

Head, K. and Mayer, T. (2014). "Chapter 3: Gravity Equations: Workhorse,Toolkit and Cookbook." In Gopinath, G., Helpman, E., and Rogoff, K., eds., *Handbook of International Economics*, volume 4 of *Handbook of International Economics*, pp. 131–195. Elsevier.

Henrekson, M. (2020). "How labor market institutions affect job creation and productivity growth." *IZA World of Labor 38*, Institute for the Study of Labor.

IMF (2013). "Balance of payments manual." Sixth edition.

Jeffreys, H. (1961). *Theory of Probability*. 3rd ed., Oxford University Press.

Kaldor, N. (1978). "The effects of devaluations on trade in manufactures." Volume 6 of *Further essays on applied economics*, pp. 99–116. Duckworth, London.

Kaltenbrunner, A. (2015). "A post Keynesian framework of exchange rate determination: A Minskyan approach." *Journal of Post Keynesian Economics*, 38(3): 426–448.

Kass, R. E. and Raftery, A. E. (1995). "Bayes Factors." *Journal of the American Statistical Association*, 90(430): 773–795.

Kolasa, M., Rubaszek, M., and Taglioni, D. (2010). "Firms in the great global recession: The role of foreign ownership and financial dependence." *Emerging Markets Review*, 11(4): 341–357.

Krueger, A. O. (2006). *A Remarkable Prospect: Opportunities and Challenges for the Modern Global Economy*. McKenna Lecture at Claremont McKenna College by Anne O. Krueger, First Deputy Managing Director, IMF; accessed 05.03.2019. https://www.imf.org/en/News/Articles/2015/09/28/04/53/sp050206.

Krugman, P. (1994). "Competitiveness: A dangerous obsession." *Foreign Affairs*, 73(2): 28–44.

Krugman, P. (1996). "Making sense of the competitiveness debate." *Oxford Review of Economic Policy*, 12(3): 17–25.

Krugman, P. R., Obstfeld, M., and Melitz, M. (2012). *International Economics*. Pearson.

Lane, P. R. and Milesi-Ferretti, G. M. (2007). "The external wealth of nations mark II: Revised and extended estimates of foreign assets and liabilities, 1970–2004." *Journal of International Economics*, 73(2): 223–250.

Ley, E. and Steel, M. F. J. (2007). "On the effect of prior assumptions in Bayesian model averaging with applications to growth regression." *Policy Research Working Paper Series 4238*, The World Bank.

Lipsey, R. (2002). "Home and Host Country Effects of FDI." *NBER Working Papers 9293*, National Bureau of Economic Research, Inc.

Llewellyn, J. (1996). "Tackling Europe's competitiveness." *Oxford Review of Economic Policy*, 12(3): 87–96.

Lucas, R. E. (1990). "Why does not capital flow from rich to poor countries?" *The American Economic Review*, 80(2): 92–96.

Ma, Y., Qu, B., and Zhang, Y. (2010). "Judicial quality, contract intensity and trade: Firm-level evidence from developing and transition countries." *Journal of Comparative Economics*, 38(2): 146–159.

MacDonald, R. (1998). "What determines real exchange rates? The long and the short of it." *Journal of International Financial Markets, Institutions and Money*, 8(2): 117–153.

Madsen, J. B. (2008). "Innovations and Manufacturing Export Performance in the OECD Countries." *Oxford Economic Papers*, 60(1): 143–167.

Magaziner, I. C. and Reich, R. B. (1982). "Minding America's business: The decline and rise of the American economy." *Politics & Society*, 11(4): 509–510.

Magnier, A. and Toujas-Bernate, J. (1994). "Technology and trade: Empirical evidence for the major five industrialized countries." *Review of World Economics*, 130(3): 494–520.

Marjit, S. and Ray, M. (2017). "Export profitability, competition and technology." *International Review of Economics & Finance*, 47(C): 35–45.

Meese, R. and Rogoff, K. (1983). "Empirical exchange rate models of the seventies: Do they fit out of sample?" *Journal of International Economics*, 14: 3–24.

Molodtsova, T. and Papell, D. H. (2009). "Out-of-sample exchange rate predictability with taylor rule fundamentals." *Journal of International Economics*, 77(2): 167–180.

Montobbio, F. and Rampa, F. (2005). "The impact of technology and structural change on export performance in nine developing countries." *World Development*, 33(4): 527–547.

Moral-Benito, E. (2012). "Determinants of Economic Growth: A Bayesian Panel Data Approach." *The Review of Economics and Statistics*, 94(2): 566–579.

Moral-Benito, E. and Roehn, O. (2016). "The impact of financial regulation on current account balances." *European Economic Review*, 81: 148–166.

Mulliqi, A., Adnett, N., and Hisarciklilar, M. (2019). “Human capital and exports: A micro-level analysis of transition countries.” *The Journal of International Trade & Economic Development*, 28(7): 775–800.

Nickell, S. J. (1981). “Biases in dynamic models with fixed effects.” *Econometrica*, 49(6): 1417–26.

North, D. C. (1989). “Institutions and economic growth: A historical introduction.” *World Development*, 17(9): 1319–1332.

Obstfeld, M. and Rogoff, K. (1995). “The intertemporal approach to the current account.” In G., M. G. and K., R., eds., *Handbook of International Economics*, Vol. 3, Ch. 34, pp. 1731–1799. Elsevier.

Obstfeld, M. and Rogoff, K. (2009). “Global Imbalances and the Financial Crisis: Products of Common Causes.” *CEPR Discussion Papers 7606*, C.E.P.R. Discussion Papers.

Ranjan, P., Hasan, R., and Eleazar, E. J. (2018). “Labor Market Regulations in the Context of Structural Transformation.” *ADB Economics Working Paper Series 543*, Asian Development Bank.

Reich, R. B. (1992). *The Work of Nations: Preparing Ourselves for 21st Century Capitalism*. Vintage.

Rodrik, D. (2008). *One Economics, Many Recipes: Globalization, Institutions, and Economic Growth*. Princeton University Press, Princeton, NJ.

Sachs, J. D. (1981). “The current account and macroeconomic adjustment in the 1970s.” *Brookings Papers on Economic Activity*, 12(1): 201–282.

Sala-I-Martin, X., Doppelhofer, G., and Miller, R. I. (2004). “Determinants of Long-Term Growth: A Bayesian Averaging of Classical Estimates (BACE) Approach.” *American Economic Review*, 94(4): 813–835.

Samuelson, P. A. (1964). “Theoretical notes on trade problems.” *The Review of Economics and Statistics*, 46(2): 145–154.

Schnatz, B., Bussière, M., and Fidrmuc, J. (2005). “Trade integration of Central and Eastern European countries: lessons from a gravity model.” *Working Paper Series 545*, European Central Bank.

Sheffrin, S. M. and Woo, W. T. (1990). “Present value tests of an intertemporal model of the current account.” *Journal of International Economics*, 29(3–4): 237–253.

Singh, T. (2007). "Intertemporal optimizing models of trade and current account balance: A survey." *Journal of Economic Surveys*, 21(1): 25–64.

Steel, M. F. J. (2017). "Model Averaging and its Use in Economics." *MPRA Paper 81568*, University Library of Munich, Germany.

Taglioni, D. and Baldwin, R. (2014). "Gravity chains: Estimating bilateral trade flows when parts and components trade is important." *Journal of Banking and Financial Economics*, 2(2): 61–82.

Taylor, J. B. (1993). "Discretion versus policy rules in practice." *Carnegie-Rochester Conference Series on Public Policy*, 39(1): 195–214.

Tyson, L. D. (1992). *Who's Bashing Whom? Trade Conflict in High Technology Industries*. Peterson Institute for International Economics.

Wakelin, K. (1998). "The role of innovation in bilateral OECD trade performance." *Applied Economics*, 30(10): 1335–1346.

Wdowiński, P. (2011). "Model monetarny kursu równowagi złoty/euro: analiza kointegracyjna." *Gospodarka Narodowa. The Polish Journal of Economics*, (3): 67–86.

Williamson, J. (1994). *Estimating Equilibrium Exchange Rates*. Peterson Institute for International Economics.

Zellner, A. (1986). *On assessing prior distributions and Bayesian regression analysis with g-prior distributions*, Ch. 15, pp. 233–243. North-Holland.

Zeugner, S. and Feldkircher, M. (2015). "Bayesian Model Averaging Employing Fixed and Flexible Priors: The BMS Package for R." *Journal of Statistical Software, Articles*, 68(4): 1–37.

7 Appendix

Table 22. Sensitivity analysis of baseline results for labour-intensive and resource-intensive manufactures' exports

	Baseline assumptions		*Conservative assumptions*		*Unconservative assumptions*	
	PIP	*Post. mean*	*PIP*	*Post. mean*	*PIP*	*Post. mean*
Price competitiveness						
Std. dev. of NEER	0.12	-0.002	0.04	-0.001	0.20	-0.002
ULC	0.08	0.002	0.02	0.001	0.13	0.003
Technological factors and human capital						
Patent applications	**1.00**	**0.245**	**1.00**	**0.249**	**1.00**	**0.243**
Potential GDP	**1.00**	**0.250**	**1.00**	**0.261**	**1.00**	**0.247**
FDI stock	**1.00**	**-0.090**	**0.99**	**-0.083**	**1.00**	**-0.092**
Capital output ratio	0.87	-0.290	0.66	-0.218	0.94	-0.309
R&D expenditure	0.82	0.111	0.53	0.072	0.92	0.126
School life expectancy	0.15	0.034	0.05	0.013	0.24	0.052
Population with tertiary education	0.08	0.000	0.02	0.001	0.13	0.000
Institutional factors						
Regulation	**1.00**	**0.864**	**1.00**	**0.863**	**1.00**	**0.863**
Sound money	**1.00**	**0.229**	**1.00**	**0.234**	**1.00**	**0.226**
Freedom to trade internationally	**0.99**	**0.920**	0.94	0.834	**1.00**	**0.944**
Legal system and property rights	0.62	-0.297	0.47	-0.256	0.72	-0.329
Size of government	0.26	0.033	0.10	0.013	0.38	0.047

Notes: PIP and Post. mean denote posterior inclusion probability and posterior mean, respectively. The results for regressors with a strong impact on exports (PIP between 0.95 and 1.00) were bolded for convenience.

Source: own elaboration.

Table 23. Sensitivity analysis of baseline results for low-skill and technology-intensive manufactures' exports

	Baseline assumptions		*Conservative assumptions*		*Unconservative assumptions*	
	PIP	*Post. mean*	*PIP*	*Post. mean*	*PIP*	*Post. mean*
Price competitiveness						
Std. dev. of NEER	0.12	-0.002	0.04	-0.001	0.20	-0.002
ULC	0.08	0.002	0.02	0.001	0.13	0.003
Technological factors and human capital						
Patent applications	**1.00**	**0.245**	**1.00**	**0.249**	**1.00**	**0.243**
Potential GDP	**1.00**	**0.250**	**1.00**	**0.261**	**1.00**	**0.247**
FDI stock	**1.00**	**-0.090**	**0.99**	**-0.083**	**1.00**	**-0.092**
Capital output ratio	0.87	-0.290	0.66	-0.218	0.94	-0.309
R&D expenditure	0.82	0.111	0.53	0.072	0.92	0.126
School life expectancy	0.15	0.034	0.05	0.013	0.24	0.052
Population with tertiary education	0.08	0.000	0.02	0.001	0.13	0.000
Institutional factors						
Regulation	**1.00**	**0.864**	**1.00**	**0.863**	**1.00**	**0.863**
Sound money	**1.00**	**0.229**	**1.00**	**0.234**	**1.00**	**0.226**
Freedom to trade internationally	**0.99**	**0.920**	0.94	0.834	**1.00**	**0.944**
Legal system and property rights	0.62	-0.297	0.47	-0.256	0.72	-0.329
Size of government	0.26	0.033	0.10	0.013	0.38	0.047

Notes: PIP and Post. mean denote posterior inclusion probability and posterior mean, respectively. The results for regressors with a strong impact on exports (PIP between 0.95 and 1.00) were bolded for convenience.

Source: own elaboration.

Table 24. Sensitivity analysis of baseline results for medium-skill and technology-intensive manufactures' exports

	Baseline assumptions		*Conservative assumptions*		*Unconservative assumptions*	
	PIP	*Post. mean*	*PIP*	*Post. mean*	*PIP*	*Post. mean*
	Price competitiveness					
Std. dev. of NEER	0.12	-0.002	0.04	-0.001	0.20	-0.002
ULC	0.08	0.002	0.02	0.001	0.13	0.003
	Technological factors and human capital					
Patent applications	**1.00**	**0.245**	**1.00**	**0.249**	**1.00**	**0.243**
Potential GDP	**1.00**	**0.250**	**1.00**	**0.261**	**1.00**	**0.247**
FDI stock	**1.00**	**-0.090**	**0.99**	**-0.083**	**1.00**	**-0.092**
Capital output ratio	0.87	-0.290	0.66	-0.218	0.94	-0.309
R&D expenditure	0.82	0.111	0.53	0.072	0.92	0.126
School life expectancy	0.15	0.034	0.05	0.013	0.24	0.052
Population with tertiary education	0.08	0.000	0.02	0.001	0.13	0.000
	Institutional factors					
Regulation	**1.00**	**0.864**	**1.00**	**0.863**	**1.00**	**0.863**
Sound money	**1.00**	**0.229**	**1.00**	**0.234**	**1.00**	**0.226**
Freedom to trade internationally	**0.99**	**0.920**	0.94	0.834	**1.00**	**0.944**
Legal system and property rights	0.62	-0.297	0.47	-0.256	0.72	-0.329
Size of government	0.26	0.033	0.10	0.013	0.38	0.047

Notes: PIP and Post. mean denote posterior inclusion probability and posterior mean, respectively. The results for regressors with a strong impact on exports (PIP between 0.95 and 1.00) were bolded for convenience.

Source: own elaboration.

Table 25. Sensitivity analysis of baseline results for high-skill and technology-intensive manufactures' exports

	Baseline assumptions		*Conservative assumptions*		*Unconservative assumptions*	
	PIP	*Post. mean*	*PIP*	*Post. mean*	*PIP*	*Post. mean*
Price competitiveness						
Std. dev. of NEER	0.12	-0.002	0.04	-0.001	0.20	-0.002
ULC	0.08	0.002	0.02	0.001	0.13	0.003
Technological factors and human capital						
Patent applications	**1.00**	**0.245**	**1.00**	**0.249**	**1.00**	**0.243**
Potential GDP	**1.00**	**0.250**	**1.00**	**0.261**	**1.00**	**0.247**
FDI stock	**1.00**	**-0.090**	**0.99**	**-0.083**	**1.00**	**-0.092**
Capital output ratio	0.87	-0.290	0.66	-0.218	0.94	-0.309
R&D expenditure	0.82	0.111	0.53	0.072	0.92	0.126
School life expectancy	0.15	0.034	0.05	0.013	0.24	0.052
Population with tertiary education	0.08	0.000	0.02	0.001	0.13	0.000
Institutional factors						
Regulation	**1.00**	**0.864**	**1.00**	**0.863**	**1.00**	**0.863**
Sound money	**1.00**	**0.229**	**1.00**	**0.234**	**1.00**	**0.226**
Freedom to trade internationally	**0.99**	**0.920**	0.94	0.834	**1.00**	**0.944**
Legal system and property rights	0.62	-0.297	0.47	-0.256	0.72	-0.329
Size of government	0.26	0.033	0.10	0.013	0.38	0.047

Notes: PIP and Post. mean denote posterior inclusion probability and posterior mean, respectively. The results for regressors with a strong impact on exports (PIP between 0.95 and 1.00) were bolded for convenience.

Source: own elaboration.

Table 26. Posterior inclusion probabilities for baseline results with interaction terms and non-linearities (dependent variable: total manufactures)

			Interaction with:													
Id	Name	-	1	2	3	4	5	6	7	8	9	10	11	12	13	14
1	Std. dev. of NEER	0.22														
2	ULC	0.05														
3	Patent applications	**1.00**														
4	Potential GDP	**1.00**														
5	FDI stock	0.30														
6	Capital output ratio	0.41														
7	School life expectancy	0.05														
8	R&D expenditure	**1.00**														
9	Population with tertiary education	0.03														
10	Regulation	0.10	0.05	**1.00**	0.11	0.63	**0.99**	0.03	0.10	0.87	0.09	0.05				
11	Sound money	0.82	0.04	0.08	0.06	0.20	0.07	0.03	0.20	0.28	0.05		0.88			
12	Freedom to trade internationally	**0.97**	0.04	0.06	0.22	**0.98**	0.17	**1.00**	0.05	0.06	027			0.25		
13	Legal system and property rights	0.54	**0.98**	0.19	0.05	0.05	0.13	0.79	0.37	0.09	0.55				0.04	
14	Size of government	0.05	0.03	0.19	0.03	0.03	**1.00**	0.03	0.24	0.03	**1.00**					**1.00**

Notes: The table shows posterior inclusion probabilities (PIP) of the different combinations of variables. The intersection between the given column ID and row ID informs on the PIP of the interaction between the two variables. The second column provides the names of the variables and the third column, denoted "-" shows the PIP of single variables (no interaction). Only square terms and interactions between the pairs of institutional and non-institutional variables and were considered.

Source: own elaboration.

Table 27. Instrumental variable (IV) estimation for potential GDP results

	Total manufactures		*LRI*		*LTI*		*MTI*		*HTI*	
	PIP	*Post. mean*	*PIP*	*Post. mean*	*PIP*	*Post. mean*	*PIP*	*Post. mean*	*PIP*	*Post. mean*
Price competitiveness										
Std. deviation of NEER	0.18	0.00	0.10	0.00	0.10	0.00	0.45	-0.02	0.28	-0.01
ULC	0.06	0.00	0.10	-0.01	0.93	-0.77	0.09	0.01	0.06	0.00
Technological factors and human capital										
Patent applications	**1.00**	**0.23**	**1.00**	**0.20**	**1.00**	**0.23**	**1.00**	**0.27**	**1.00**	**0.25**
Potential GDP	**1.00**	**0.47**	0.08	0.00	0.99	0.55	**1.00**	**0.46**	**1.00**	**0.90**
FDI stock	**1.00**	**-0.09**	**1.00**	**-0.21**	**1.00**	**0.18**	**1.00**	**-0.20**	**0.99**	**-0.11**
Capital output ratio	0.27	-0.06	0.22	-0.04	0.10	0.02	0.09	0.01	0.09	-0.01
R&D expenditure	0.32	0.03	**0.97**	**-0.18**	**0.99**	**0.28**	0.89	0.16	**0.99**	**0.26**
School life expectancy	0.07	0.00	0.62	-0.31	0.93	0.86	0.08	0.00	0.06	0.00
Population with tertiary education	0.07	0.00	**0.99**	**-0.26**	**0.99**	**-0.41**	0.12	0.01	0.26	0.04
Institutional factors										
Regulation	**1.00**	**0.83**	**1.00**	**0.92**	0.17	0.06	**1.00**	**1.15**	**1.00**	**0.92**
Sound money	**0.96**	**0.18**	**0.99**	**0.28**	0.09	-0.01	**1.00**	**0.46**	0.06	0.00
Freedom to Trade Internationally	**1.00**	**1.11**	0.82	-0.68	0.12	0.05	**1.00**	**1.63**	**1.00**	**2.37**
Legal system and property rights	0.89	-0.55	0.13	-0.04	0.88	-0.90	0.10	-0.02	0.97	-0.97
Size of government	0.24	0.04	**1.00**	**0.42**	0.12	-0.02	**0.97**	**0.38**	0.11	0.02

Note: In the first stage estimation (without model averaging) the lagged potential GDP is used as an instrument for potential GDP.

Source: own elaboration.

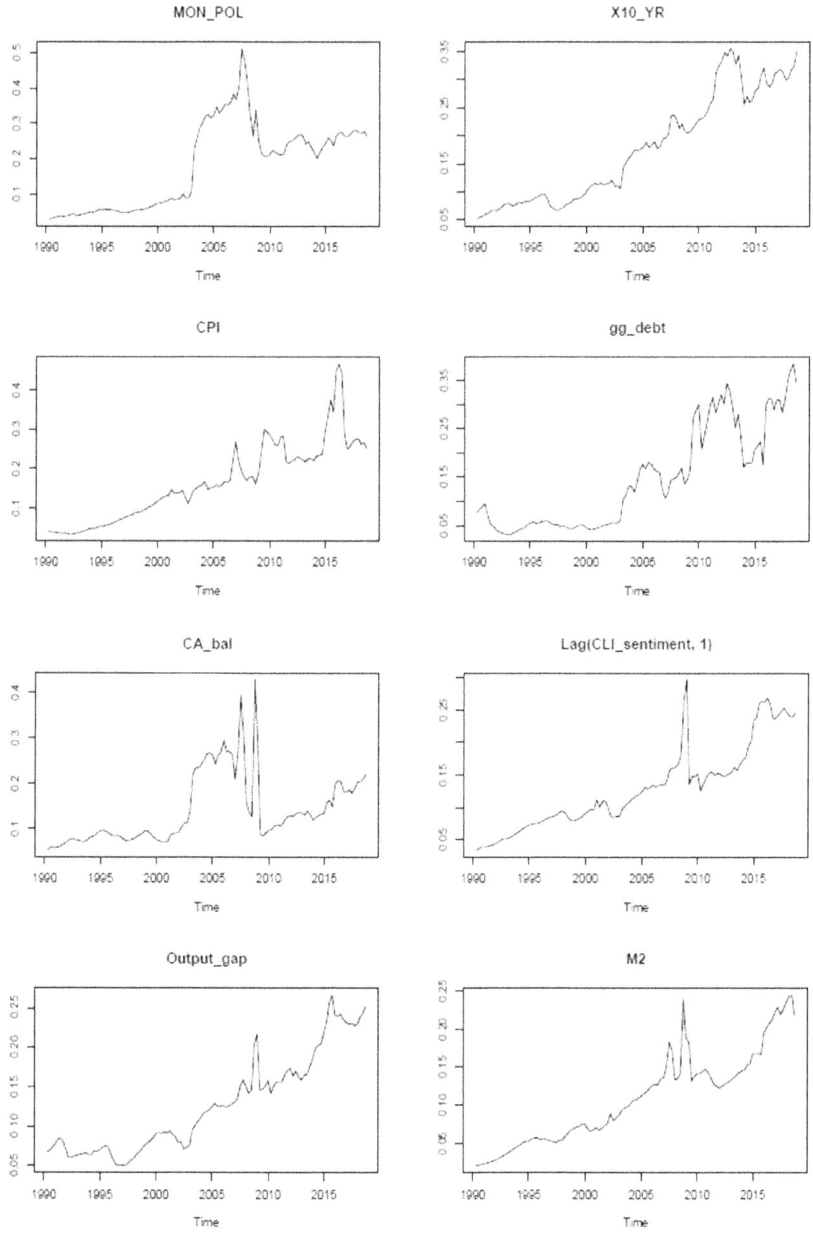

Figure 22. Posterior inclusion probabilities of additional variables for USD/CAD exchange rate forecasts
Source: own elaboration.

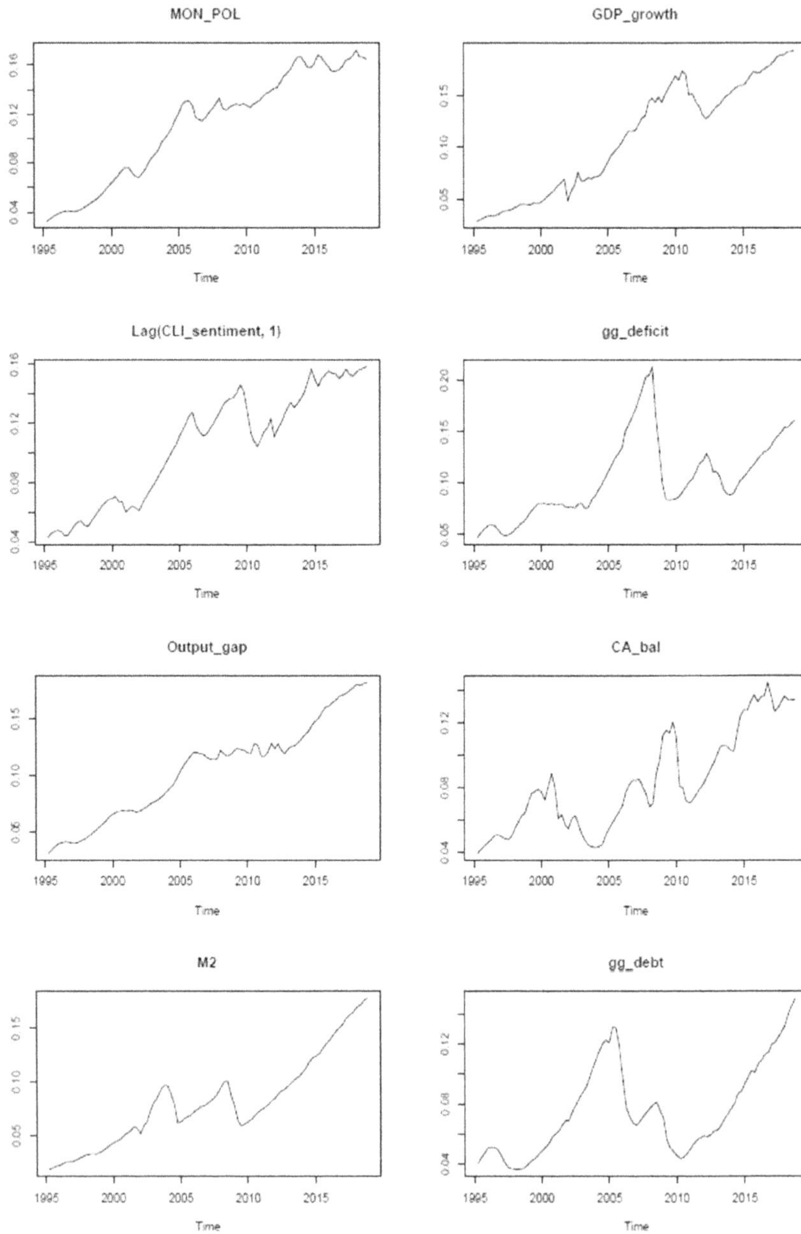

Figure 23. Posterior inclusion probabilities of additional variables for USD/CHF exchange rate forecasts
Source: own elaboration

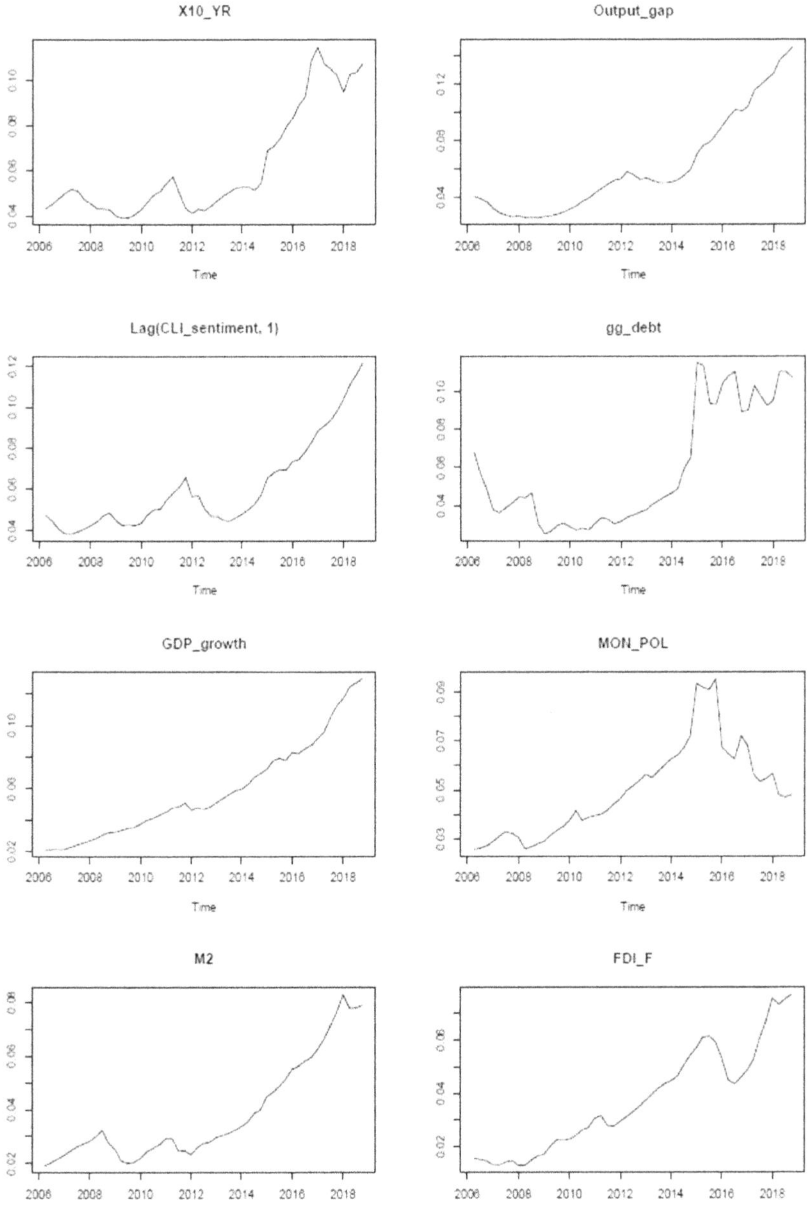

Figure 24. Posterior inclusion probabilities of additional variables for EUR/USD exchange rate forecasts
Source: own elaboration

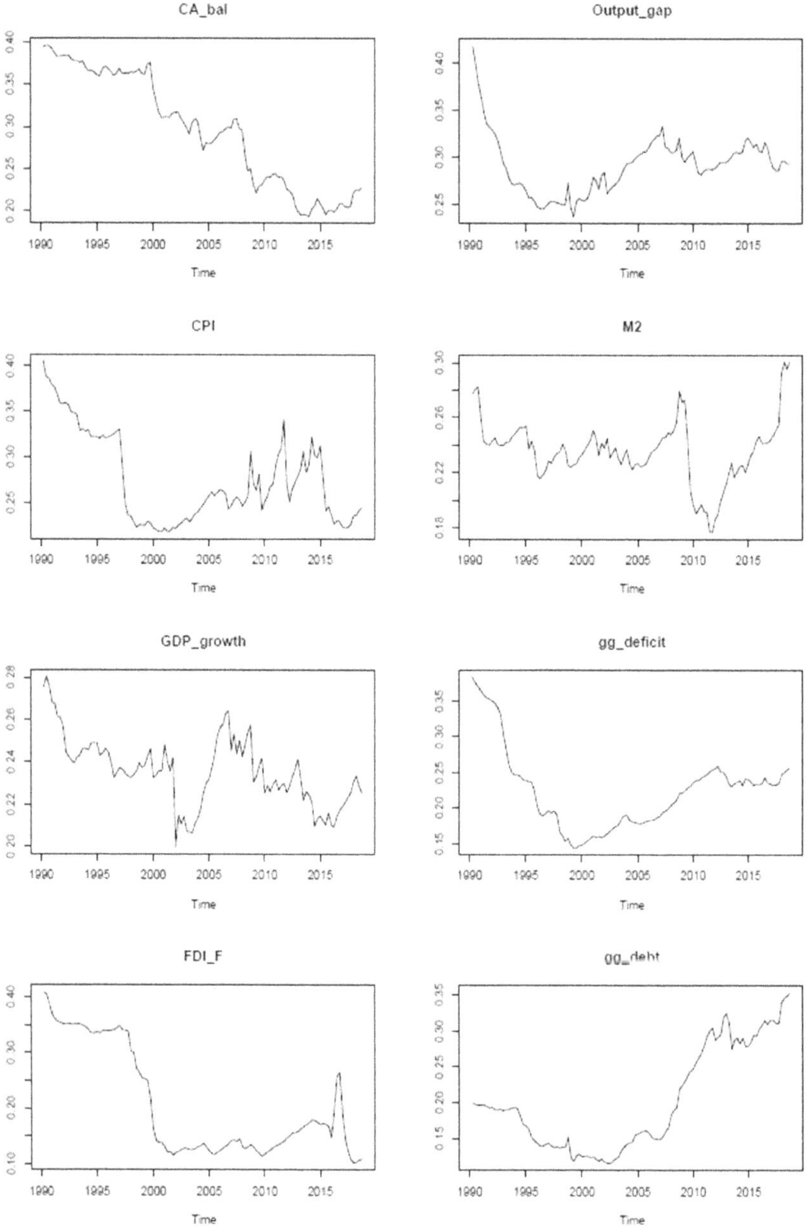

Figure 25. Posterior inclusion probabilities of additional variables for USD/JPY exchange rate forecasts
Source: own elaboration

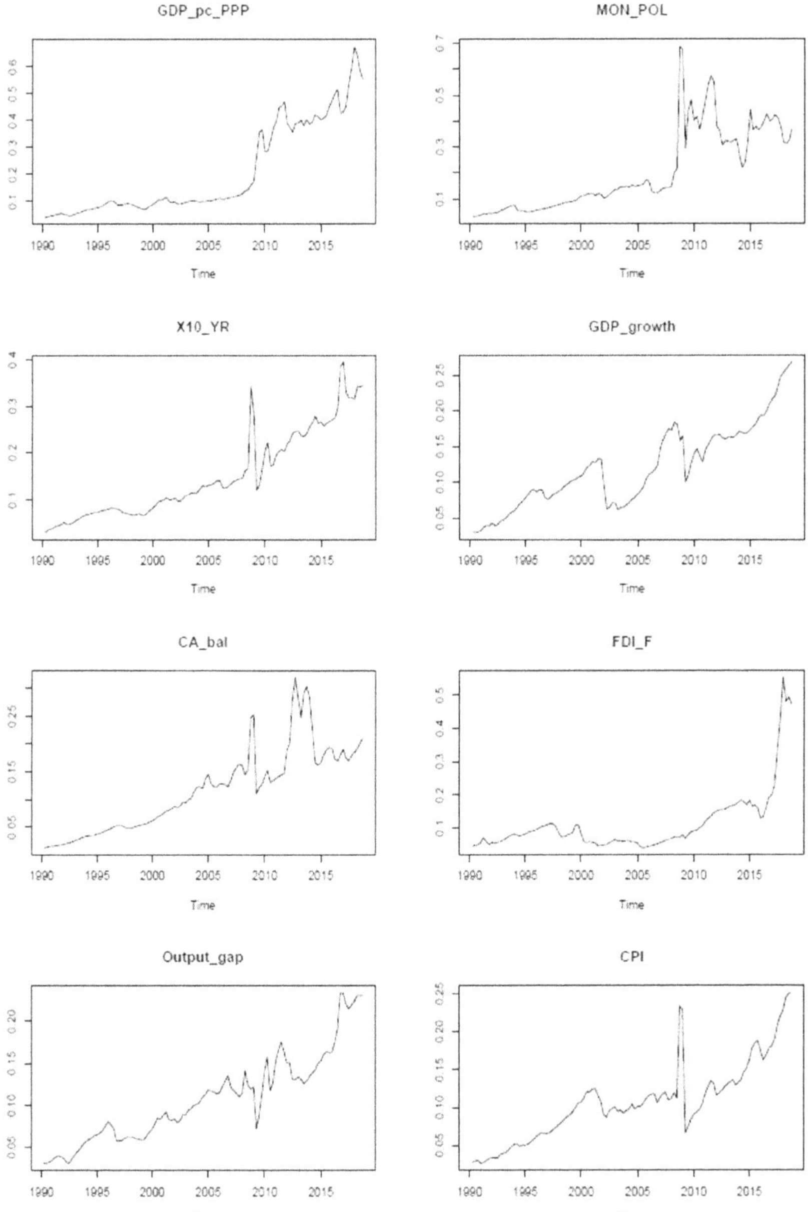

Figure 26. Posterior inclusion probabilities of additional variables for USD/GBP exchange rate forecasts
Source: own elaboration.

Index of Names

Polish Studies in Economics

Edited by Ryszard Kokoszczyński

Volume 1 Wojciech Grabowski: Employee Stock Options, Payout Policy, and Stock Returns. Shareholders and Option Holders in Large U.S. Technology Corporations. 2012.

Volume 2 Jan Jakub Michałek / Michał Brzozowski / Andrzej Cieślik (eds.): The Relationship between Human Development, Exports and Foreign Direct Investments in Emerging Europe. 2013.

Volume 3 Tomasz Żylicz: The Economics of International Environmental Cooperation. 2015.

Volume 4 Juliusz Jabłecki / Ryszard Kokoszczyński / Paweł Sakowski / Robert Ślepaczuk / Piotr Wójcik: Volatility as an Asset Class. Obvious Benefits and Hidden Risks. 2015.

Volume 5 Janusz Kudła / Konrad Walczyk / Robert Kruszewski / Katarzyna Kopczewska / Agata Kocia: Modeling Fiscal Policy in the European Union. 2015.

Volume 6 Andrzej Cieślik / Jan Jakub Michałek (eds.): Liberalization of Transportation Services in the EU: the Polish Perspective. 2015.

Volume 7 Katarzyna Metelska-Szaniawska: Economic Effects of Post-Socialist Constitutions 25 Years from the Outset of Transition. The Constitutional Political Economy Approach. 2016.

Volume 8 Elżbieta Czarny / Andżelika Kuźnar / Jerzy Menkes (eds.): The Impact of the Transatlantic Trade and Investment Partnership on International Cooperation. 2017.

Volume 9 Adam Czarnecki: Going Local? Linking and Integrating Second-Home Owners with the Community's Economy. A Comparative Study between Finnish and Polish Second-Home Owners. 2017.

Volume 10 Adam Biela (ed.): European Questionnaire for Job Analysis (EQJA). 2018.

Volume 11 Gabriela Grotkowska: Public-Sector Wage Premium in Poland. 2018.

Volume 12 Piotr Dybka: What Determines International Competitiveness of the Economy? Evidence from Bayesian Model Averaging. 2022.

www.peterlang.com

www.ingramcontent.com/pod-product-compliance
Ingram Content Group UK Ltd.
Pitfield, Milton Keynes, MK11 3LW, UK
UKHW021833100926
8556IPUK00004B/315

9 783631 856512